The Work
and the Water

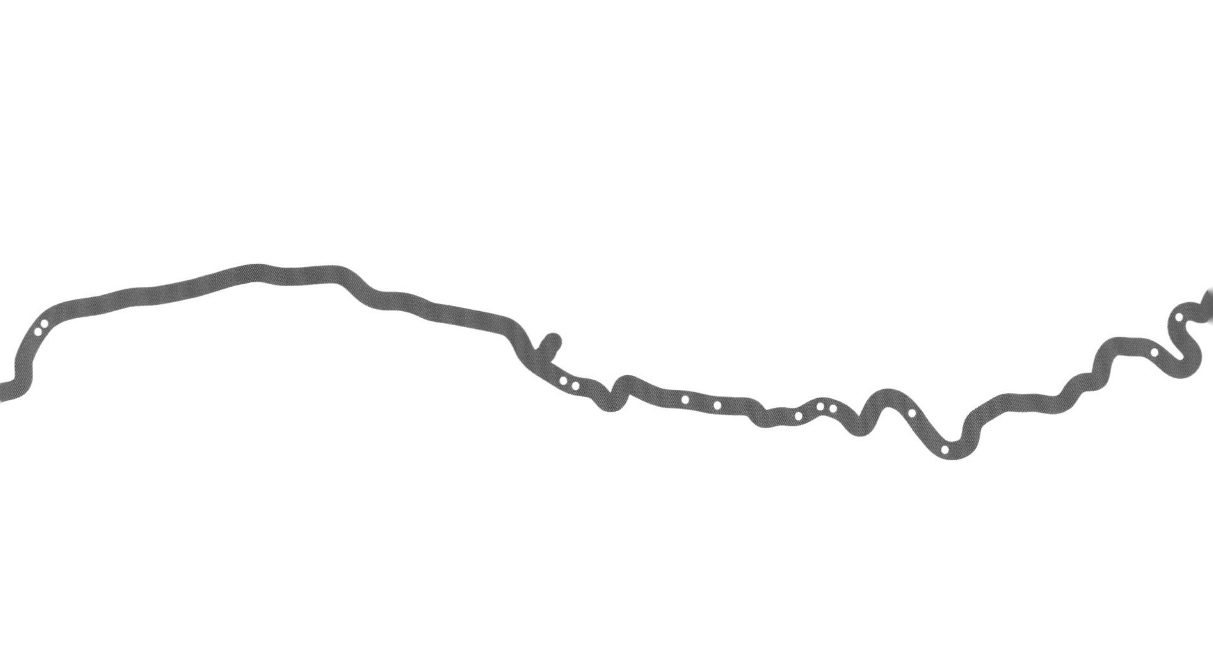

The Work and the Water

Matthew López-Jensen

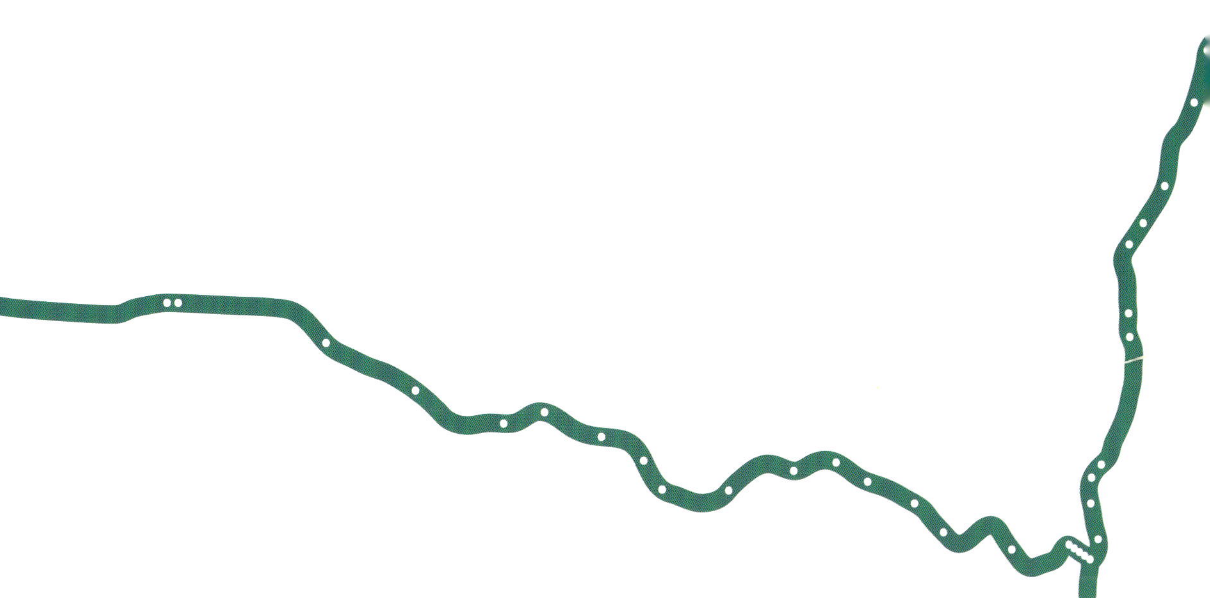

Labor and Landscapes
Along the Erie Canal

Art/Work

Kim Biel

The Voice of Labor
Along the Erie Canal

Samuel Johnson's 1755 *Dictionary of the English Language* defined a canal as "any tract or course of water made by art." In the eighteenth century, the implicit contrast in this definition was with nature. Canals are the result of human effort, labor, and engineering, while a river is a naturally occurring watercourse. More than fifty years before work began on the Erie Canal, Johnson was thinking of Dutch canals and the inland waterways that were painstakingly dug around Great Britain at the dawn of the Industrial Revolution. And yet, then as now, travelers on the Erie Canal tend not to see this effort, neither its construction nor its ongoing maintenance. Artist Matthew López-Jensen's *The Work and the Water* makes that absence felt and gives voice to the workers who made and continue to make the water's smooth passage possible over the last two hundred years.

To commemorate the opening of the Erie Canal in 1825, DeWitt Clinton, governor of New York, poured a barrel of water from Lake Erie into New York Harbor. The Canal was understood to speed and ease passage from what was then considered "the West," the Northwest Territory, and the Great Lakes, to the eastern seaboard. The Canal effectively erased the rough corduroy roads and dense forests of the region. It enabled the literal flow of goods, transforming New York Harbor into the young nation's most important port.

The opening celebration also selectively erased some of the labor that built the Canal. An artisans' festival saw members of New York City's craft associations marching triumphantly in the streets, including shipwrights and caulkers, masons and stone cutters, even coopers and comb makers, but none of the laborers who dug the Canal.[1] The festival celebrated skilled labor, not the mostly Irish working-class "navvies," or canal diggers. The Canal may have been described as a feat of engineering, but building it was equally a feat of strength and shovels.

Early travelers on the Erie Canal were overwhelmed by the beauty of the scenery, which seemed to unfurl like a painted panorama. "I cannot conceive a more beautiful combination of verdure," wrote the British Royal Navy officer Basil Hall of the Mohawk Valley in his 1828 American travelogue, concluding, "The scene looked really one of enchantment."[2] Just five years later, Thomas Hamilton, a Scottish aristocrat, admired the "fine proportion of the different features of the landscape," claiming, "The Hudson, in truth, is one of nature's felicities. Every thing

1   Sean Wilentz, "Artisan Republican Festivals and the Rise of Class Conflict in New York City, 1788–1837," in *Working-Class America: Essays on Labor, Community, and American Society*, ed. Michael H. Frisch and Daniel J. Walkowitz (Urbana: University of Illinois Press, 1983), 51–52.

2   Roger W. Hecht, ed., *The Erie Canal Reader, 1790–1950* (Syracuse, NY: Syracuse University Press, 2003), 35.

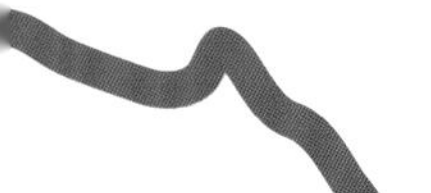

3   Ibid., 49.

4   Jane Austen, *Northanger Abbey*, ed. Susan Fraiman (New York: W. W. Norton, 2004), 75.

[*sic*] is in its proper place, and of the dimensions most proper to contribute to the general effect."[3] Many British travelers compared the landscape to art, breathing North American life into Jane Austen's description in *Northanger Abbey* of characters who viewed "the country with the eyes of persons accustomed to drawing."[4] The Canal, it seemed, had transformed nature into art.

However, travelers often struggled to reconcile what they observed from the deck of the canal boats with the social experience onboard. While British passengers focused on the lack of decorum among American travelers, American writers Nathanial Hawthorne and Herman Melville emphasized the rough culture of the "canallers" or boatmen. It was here, on deck, that writers tended to see—and especially to hear—the ongoing labor of the Canal. The frequent warning of "low bridge" was a refrain that appeared in every period account of the Canal.

This call has even lodged itself in my memory, like an echo of the past rising up out of the water. I was born in Albany. When I was a toddler, my family moved west toward Buffalo and then returned to Albany a few years later. The east-west movement of the Canal felt personal to me. In school we learned the popular song, "Low Bridge, Everybody Down." Although it sounds like a work song, mimicking the slow, walking pace of mules pulling barges, it was published in 1913, long after the Canal's heyday.

> *I've got an old mule and her name is Sal*
> *Fifteen years on the Erie Canal*
> *We've hauled some barges in our day*
> *Filled with lumber, coal, and hay*
> *And ev'ry inch of the way I know*
> *From Albany to Buffalo.*

As in López-Jensen's photographs, the voice of human labor is anonymous in the lyrics. Only the work remains. But the tempo moves my body. Its ambling beat is perfectly matched for effort. It still comes to me often, especially while hiking, although my path has taken me far from upstate New York. The singer of the song, no matter how distant from the Canal's nineteenth-century context, becomes the worker, as does the reader of the workers' words in López-Jensen's book.

The Canal in Pictures

Shortly after the Erie Canal opened, the new medium of photography was also redefining the relationship between nature and art. Like the Canal, it promised to speed up progress thanks to a mechanical intervention in nature. With the aid of a photograph, an artist could capture myriad details of a landscape in mere minutes. Photography was, as Edgar Allan Poe wrote in 1840, "*infinitely* more accurate in its representation than any painting by human hands."[5] It was like vision itself.

Soon, artists put this new way of seeing to work. They recorded the old lifeways that were being replaced by mechanized equipment and urbanization. The British duo Robert Adamson and David Octavius Hill depicted fishing communities in Newhaven, Sussex, placing people in the landscape in the picturesque mode described by Thomas Hamilton. Peter Henry Emerson turned his soft-focus lens on the farmers of marshy Norfolk. His titles described the work in a generalized way, such as *Poling the Marsh Hay* or *Haymaker with Rake*. The photographs were not meant to represent individuals so much as types, just as travelers like Hamilton and Hall sought out a general sense of "Americanness" when admiring the scenery along the Erie Canal.

Although photography promised specificity, the words that accompanied photographs throughout the nineteenth century mostly offered abstractions. Not until the 1930s would words and images align in the work of Dorothea Lange and Paul Taylor. Their 1938 book *An American Exodus*, which featured images of displaced farmers in the wake of the Dust Bowl, included quotes from the people pictured in Lange's photographs. As the duo wrote in their introduction, "In the situations which we describe are living participants who can speak.... So far as possible we have let them speak to you face to face."[6]

Photographs began speaking face-to-face and ever more insistently in the second half of the century. Danny Lyon tape-recorded lengthy interviews with members of the Chicago Outlaws Motorcycle Club beginning in 1963 and published long transcriptions in his 1968 book *The Bikeriders*. The San Franciscans photographed by Jim Goldberg for his series *Rich and Poor* wrote their own descriptions of themselves. Their words, in their own handwriting, accompanied the images in the publication of his book in 1985.

5   Edgar Allan Poe, "The Daguerreotype," *Alexander's Weekly Messenger*, January 15, 1840, 2.

6   Dorothea Lange and Paul S. Taylor, *An American Exodus: A Record of Human Erosion* (New York: Reynal & Hitchcock, 1939).

López-Jensen's photographs are related to, but also a departure from, these image-text pioneers. Here the Canal itself sings, but in a chorus of human voices. By adding words to the waterway, López-Jensen allows workers' voices to stand, finally, as the creators of the Erie Canal. As opposed to the nineteenth-century pastoral vision of the waterway, which imagined that it had arisen spontaneously from the landscape, López-Jensen reminds us that the art of the Canal is made by workers: they are its artists.

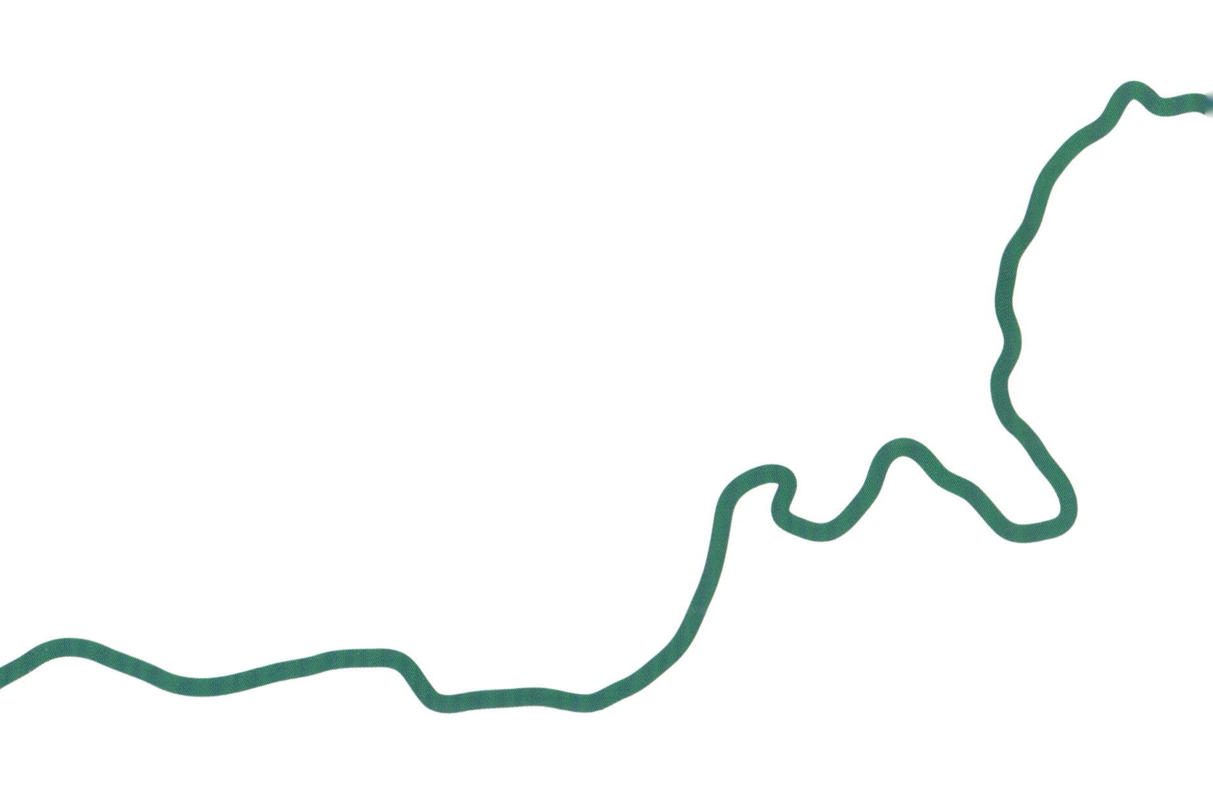

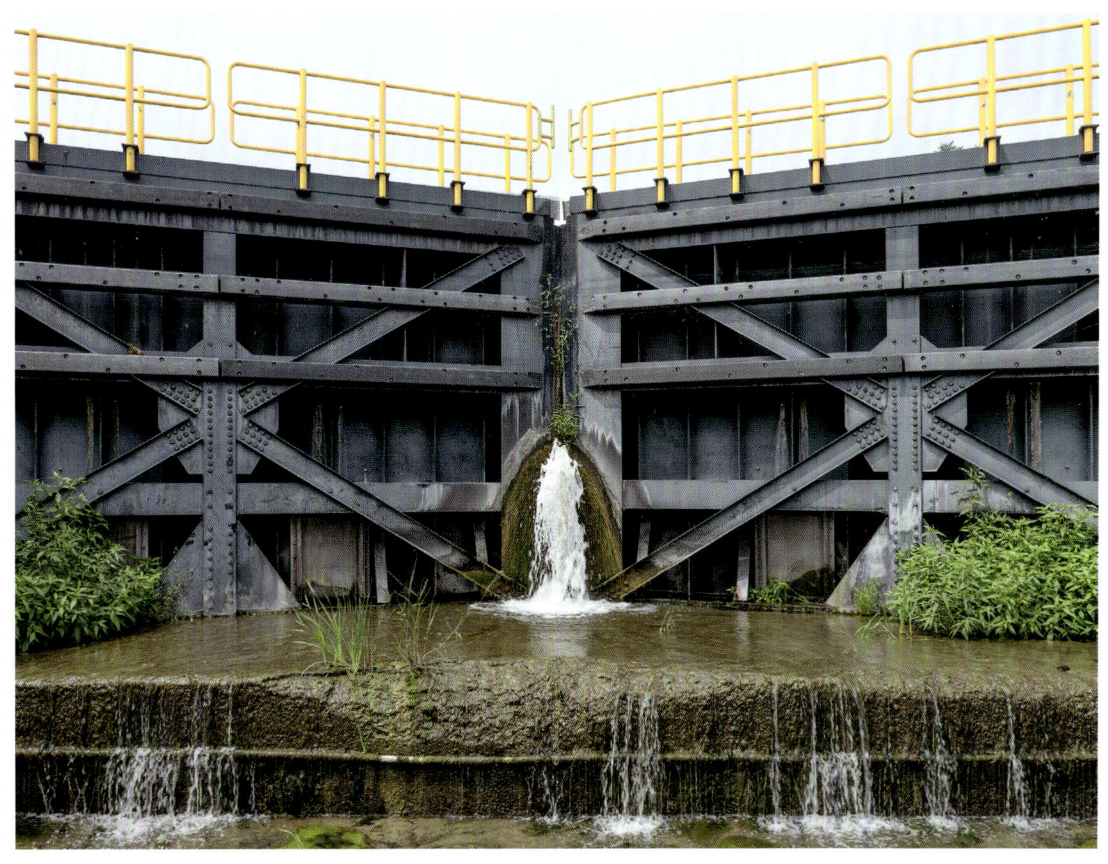

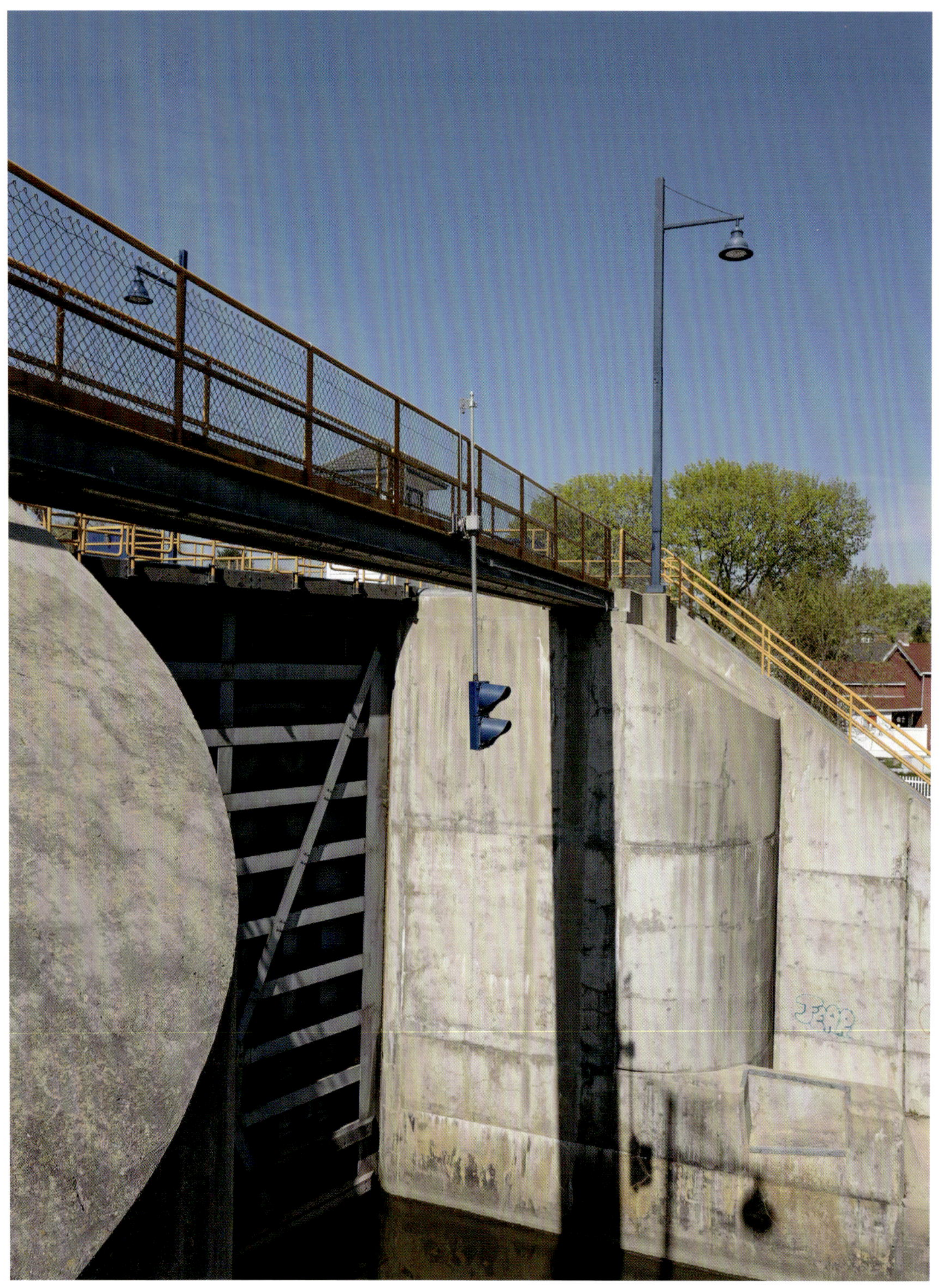

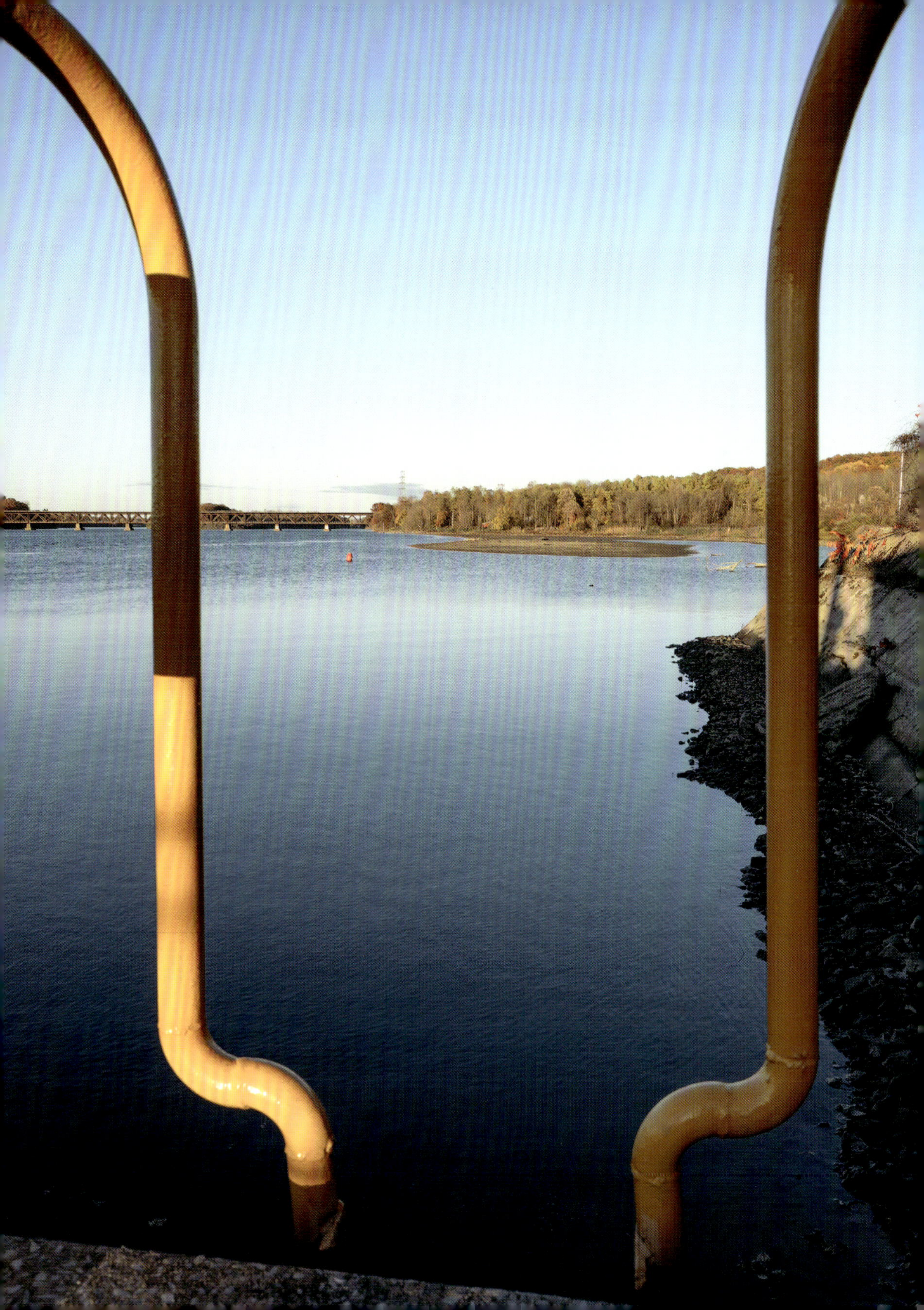

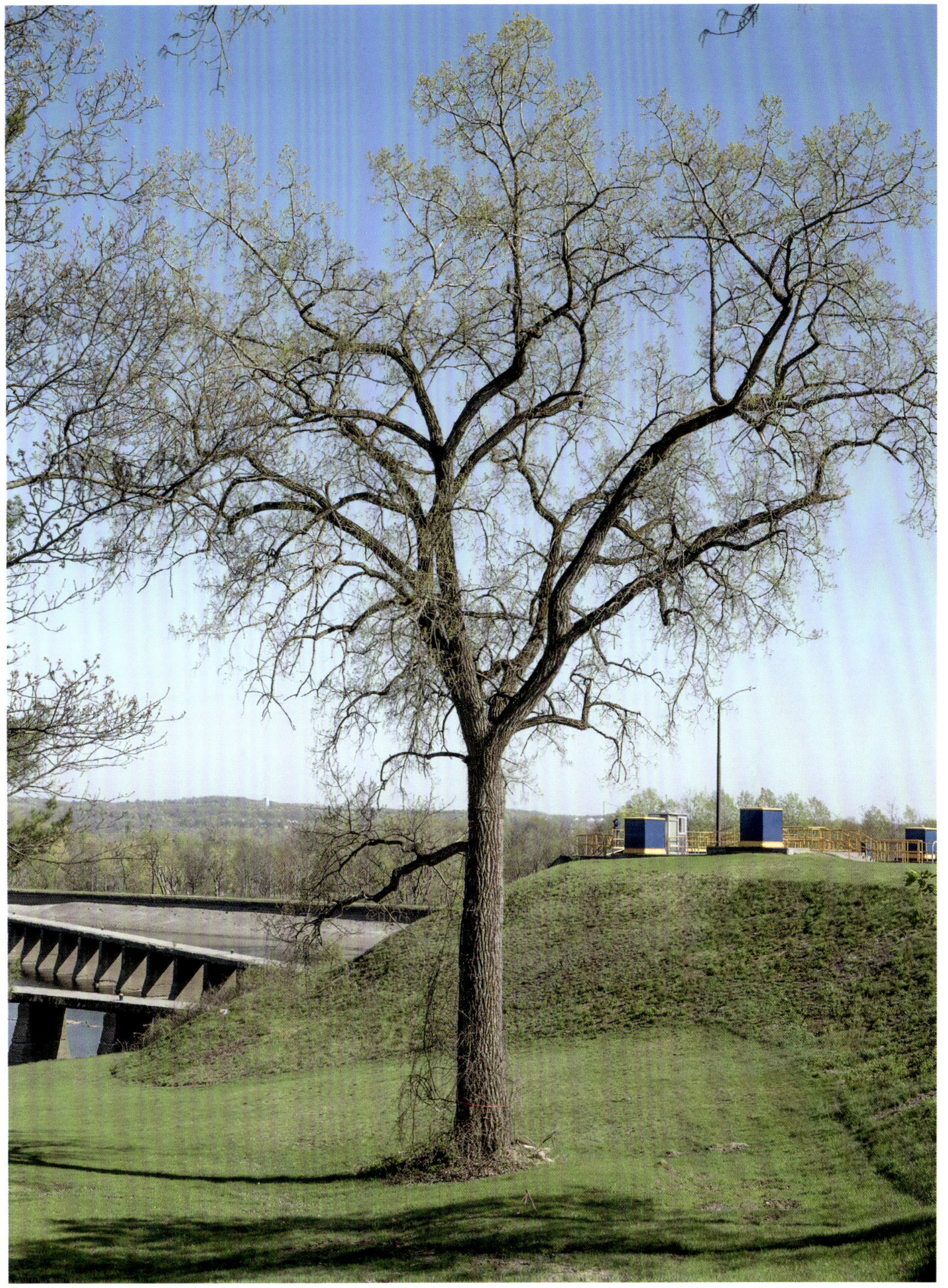

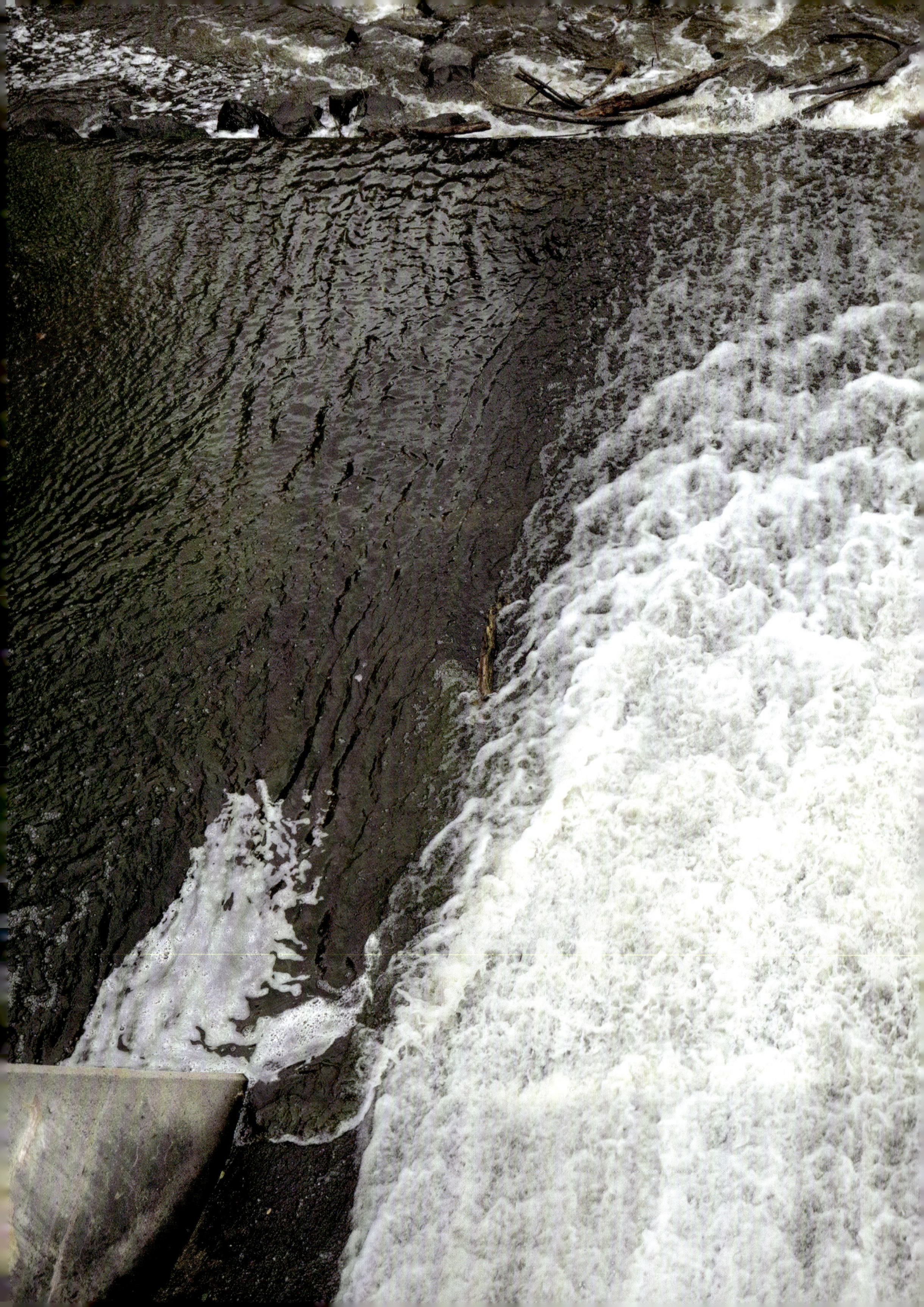

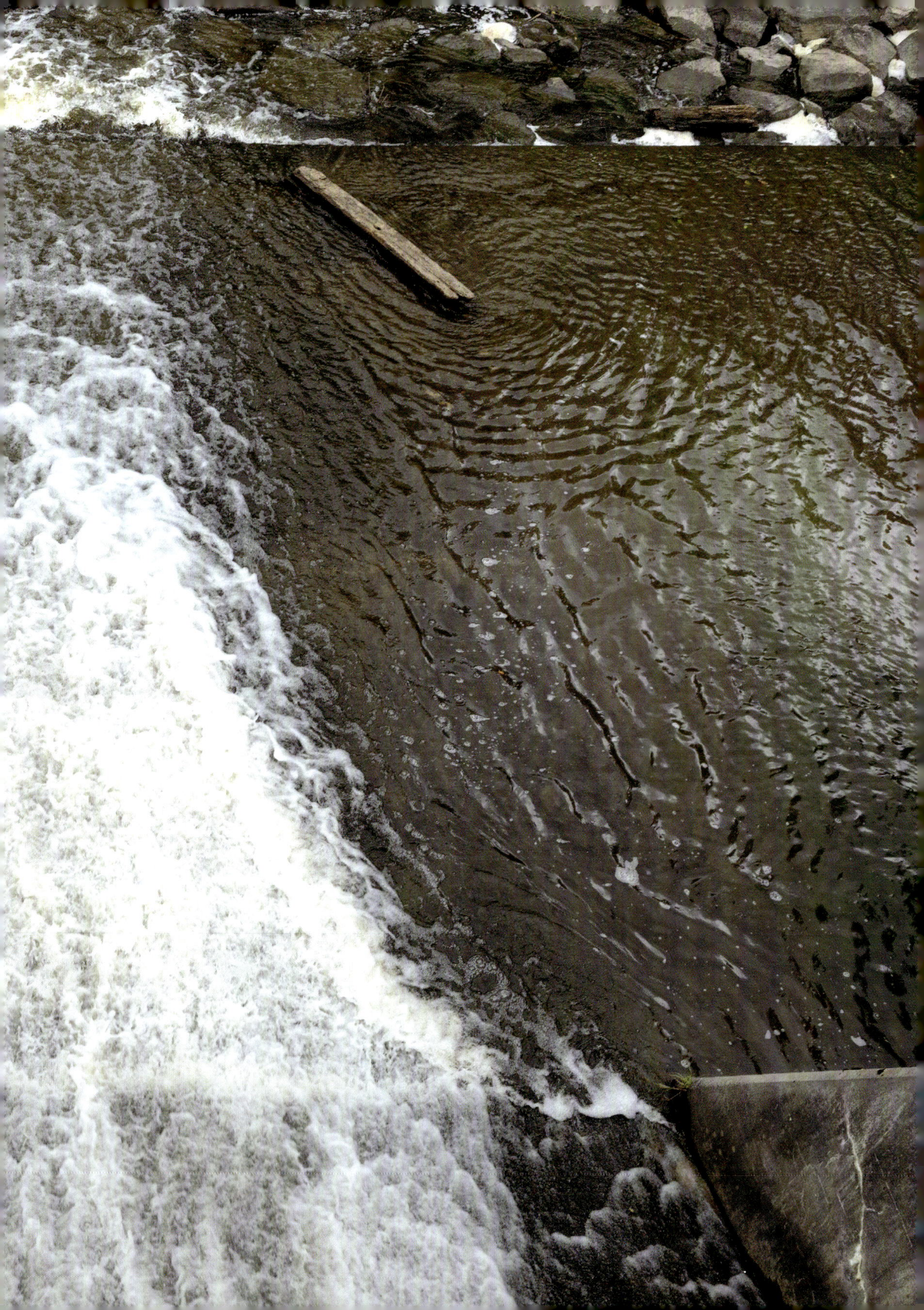

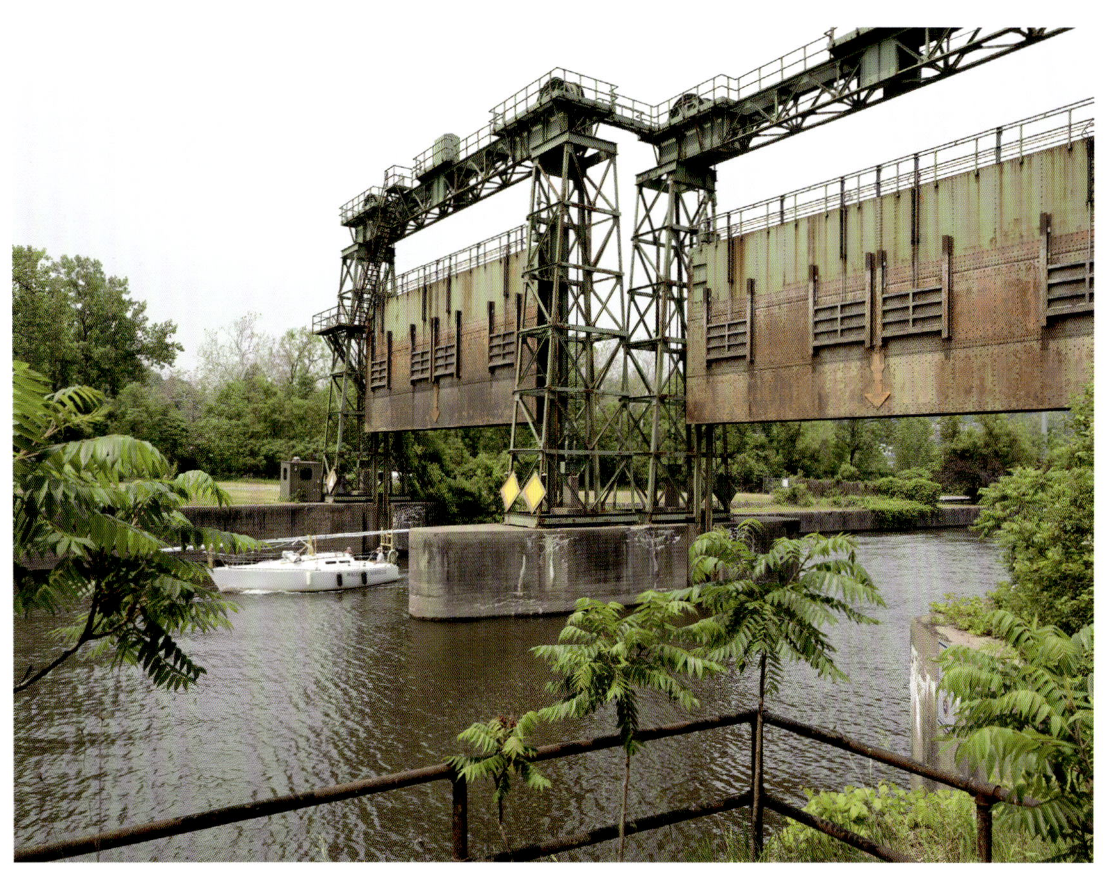

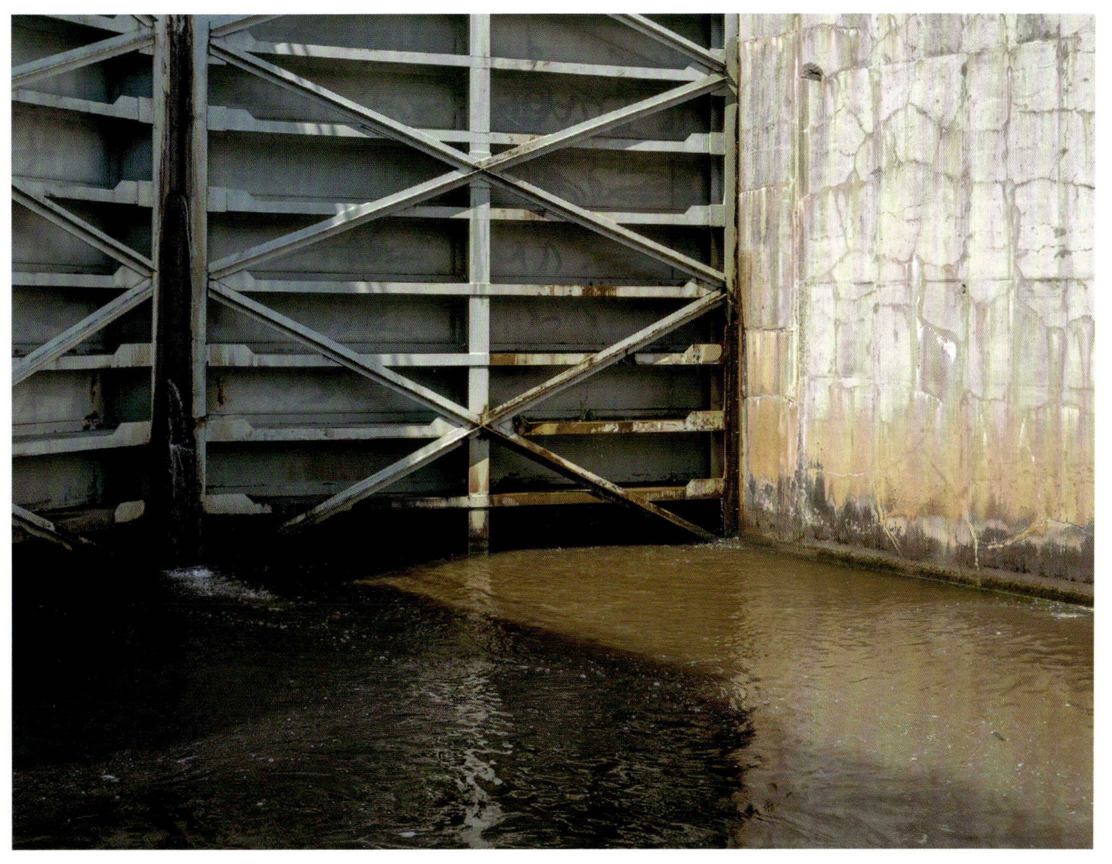

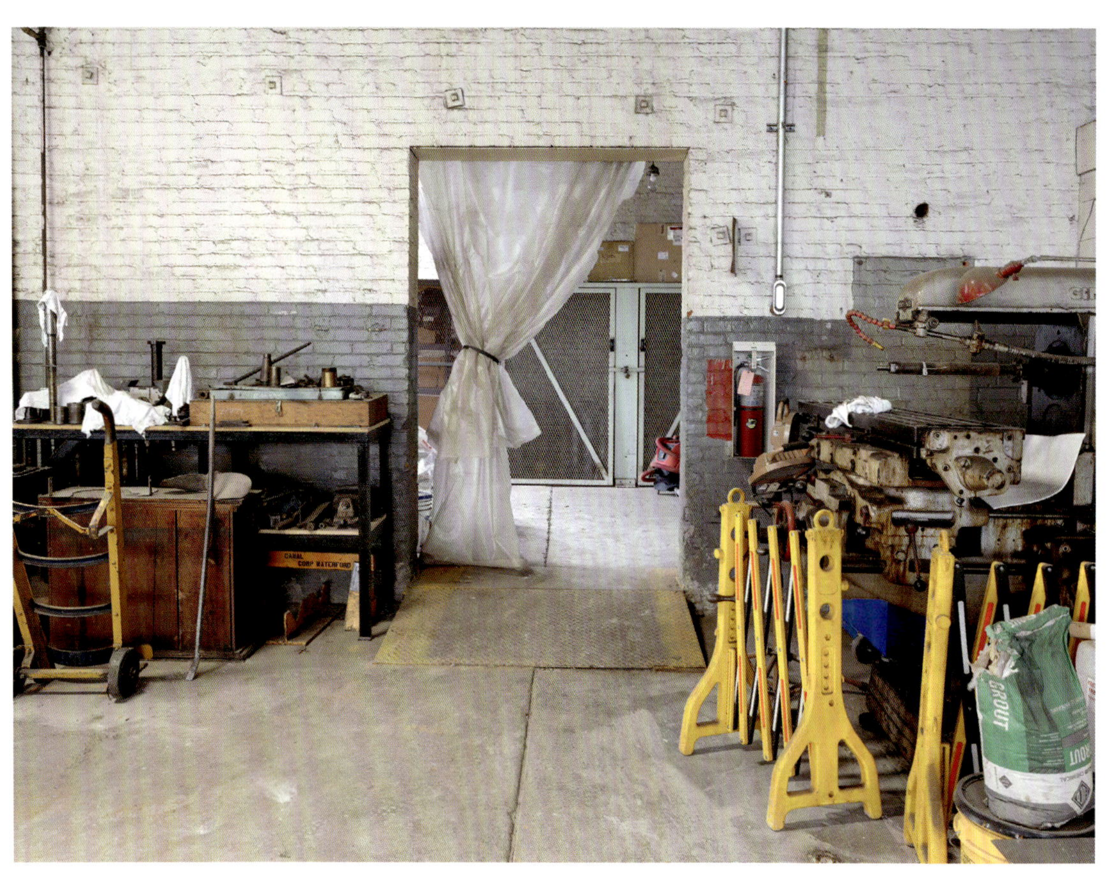

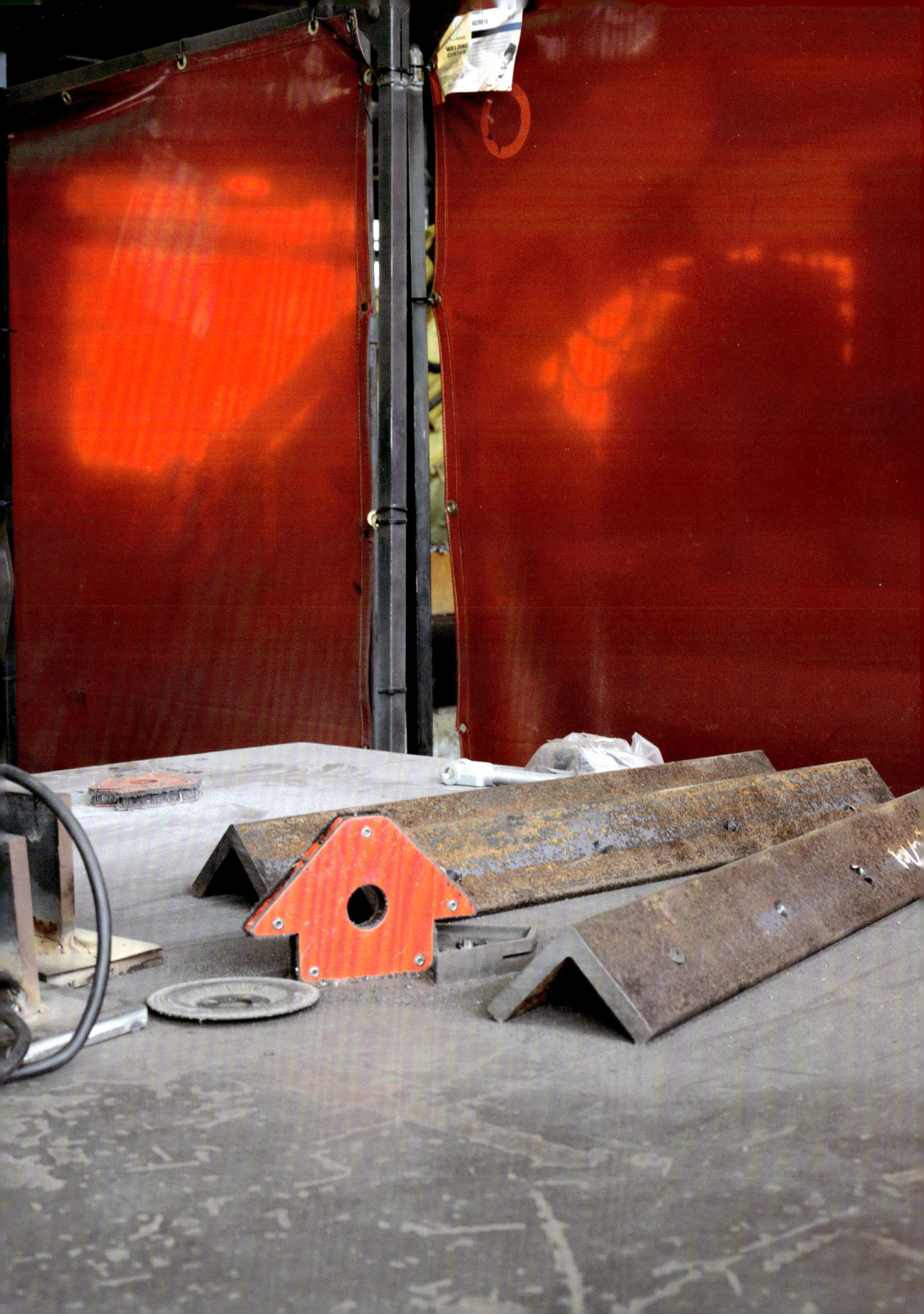

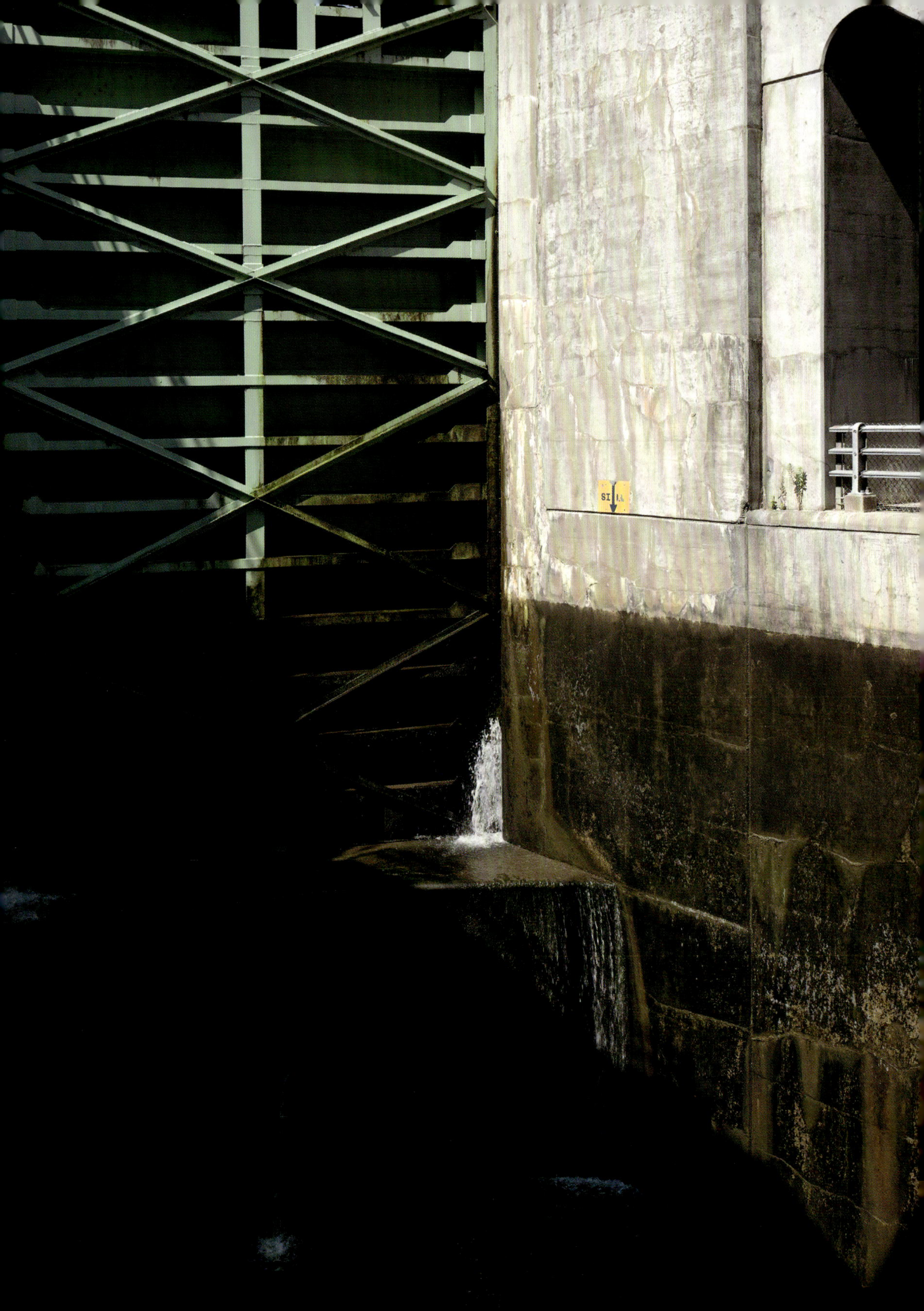

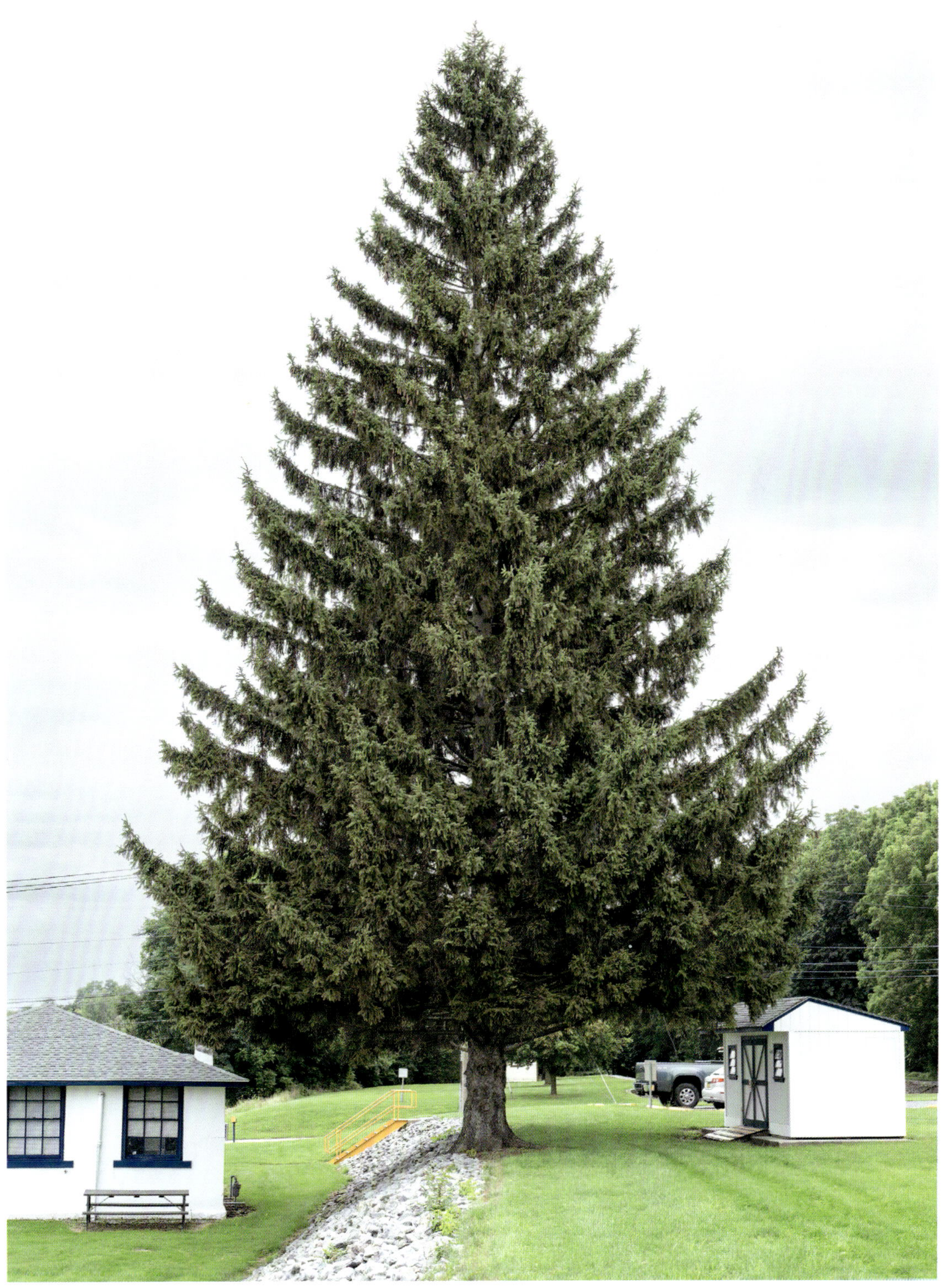

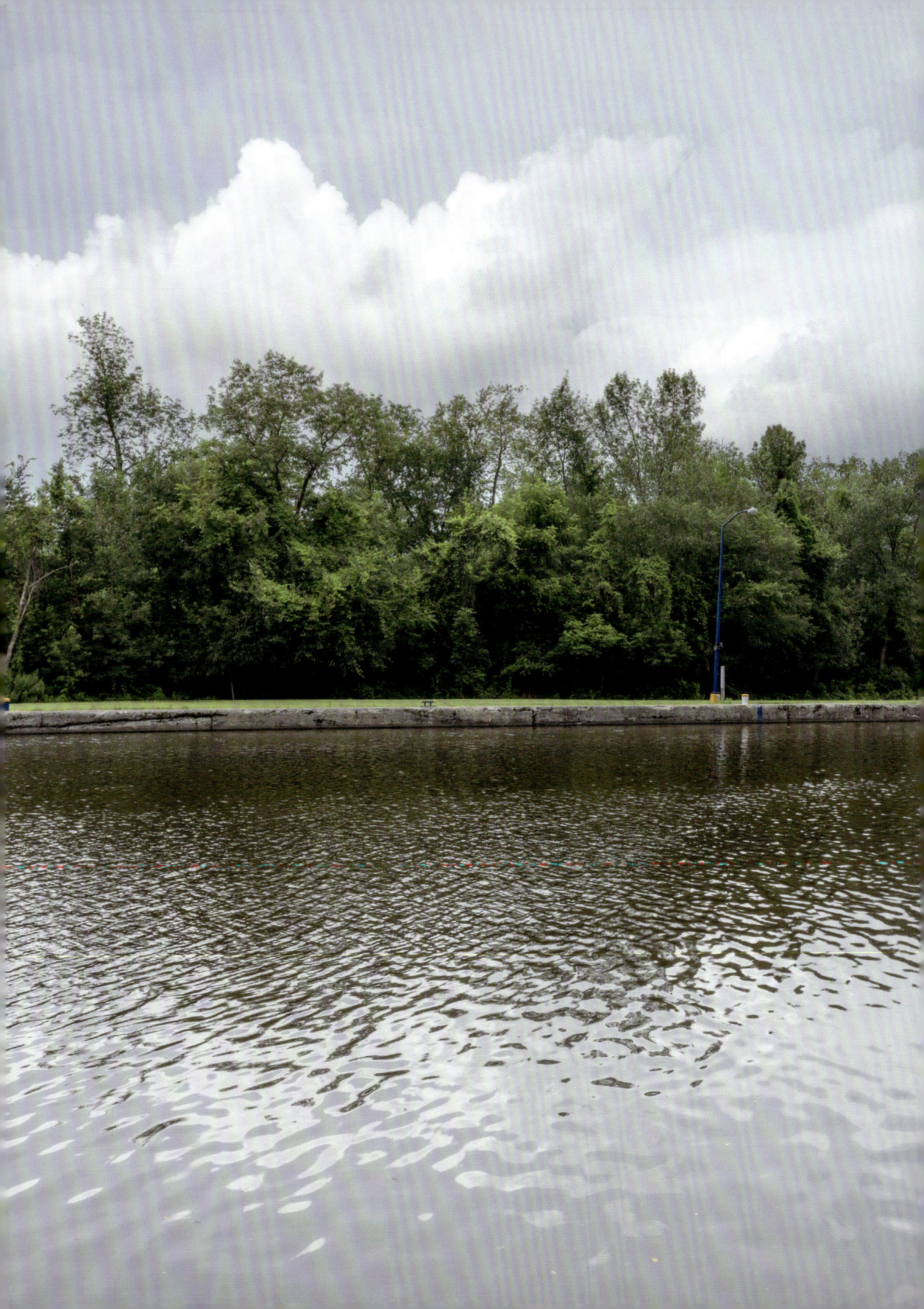

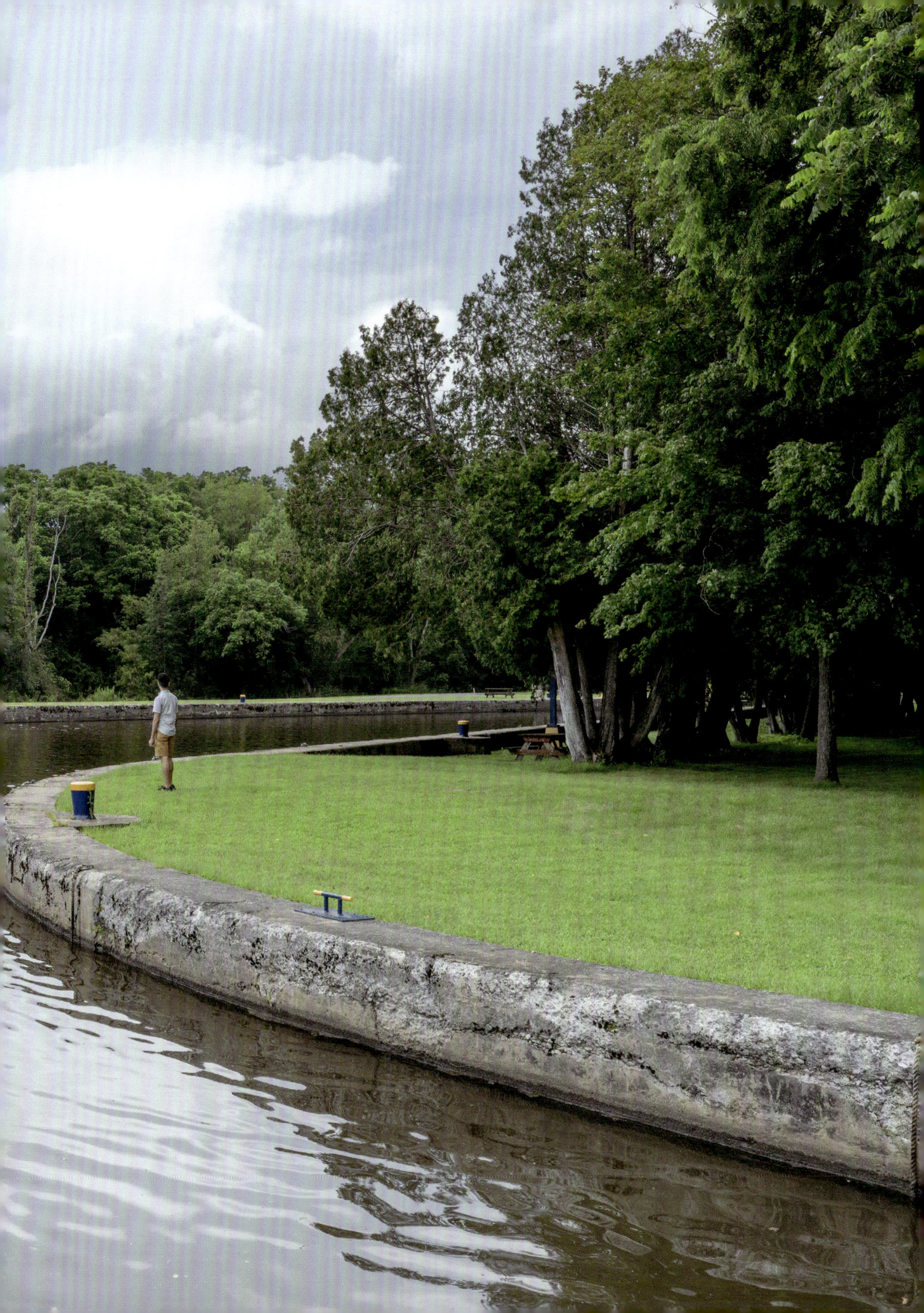

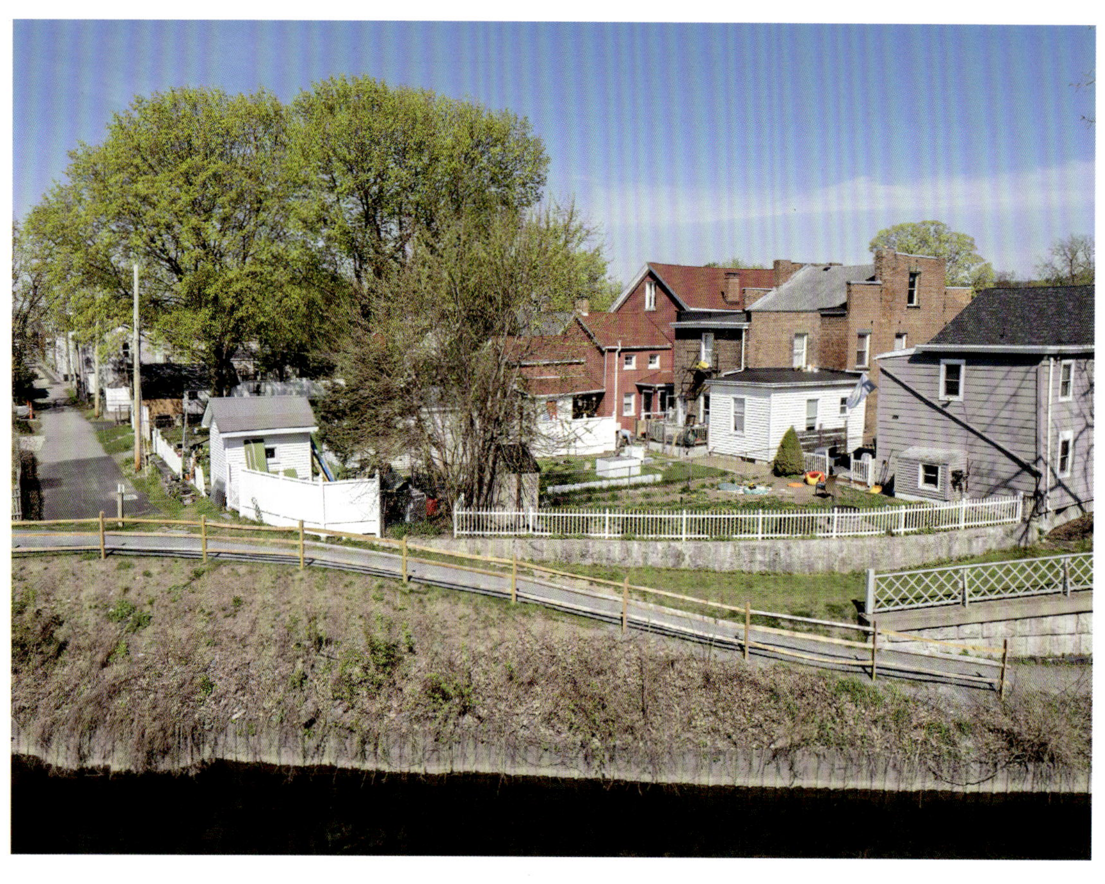

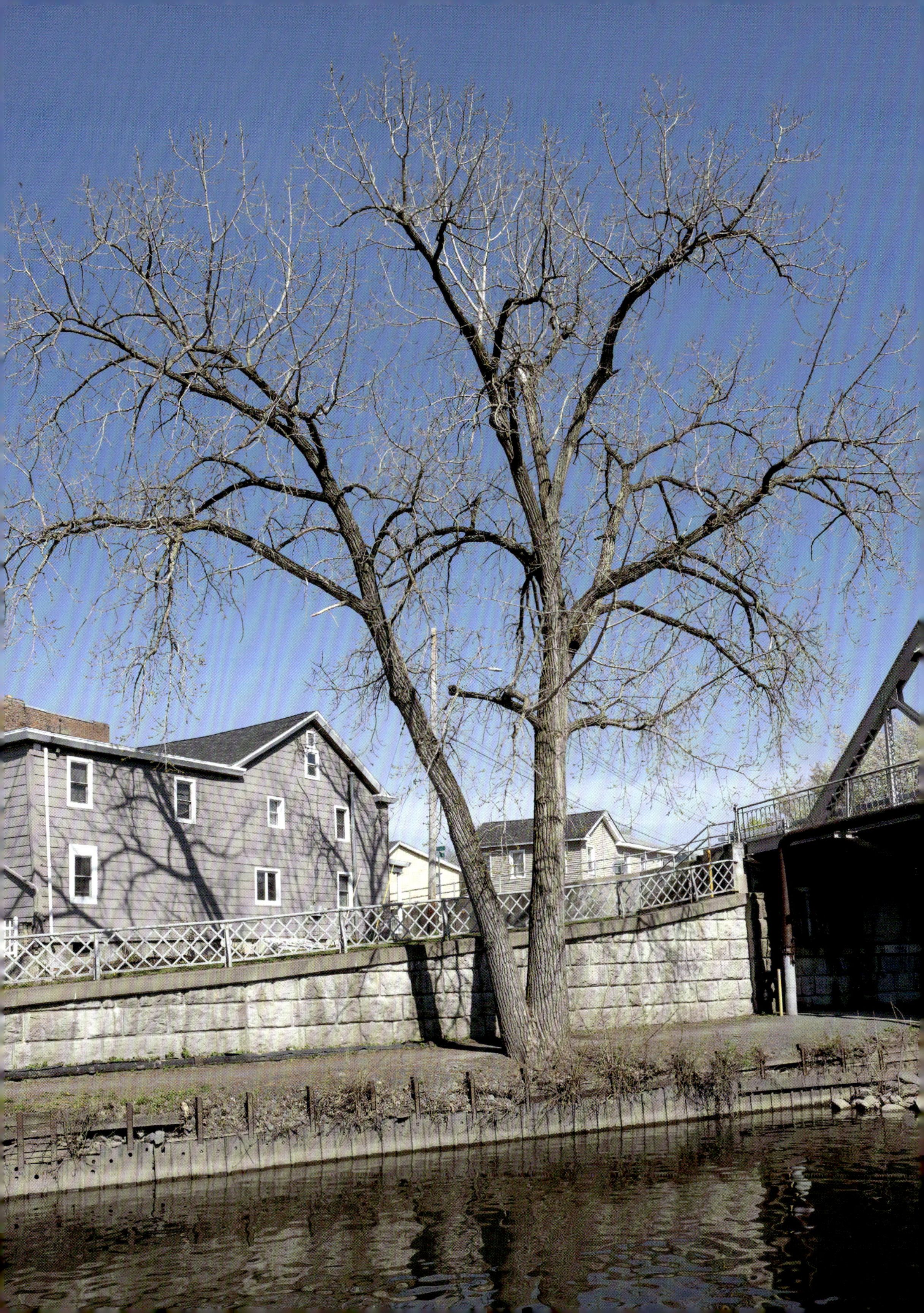

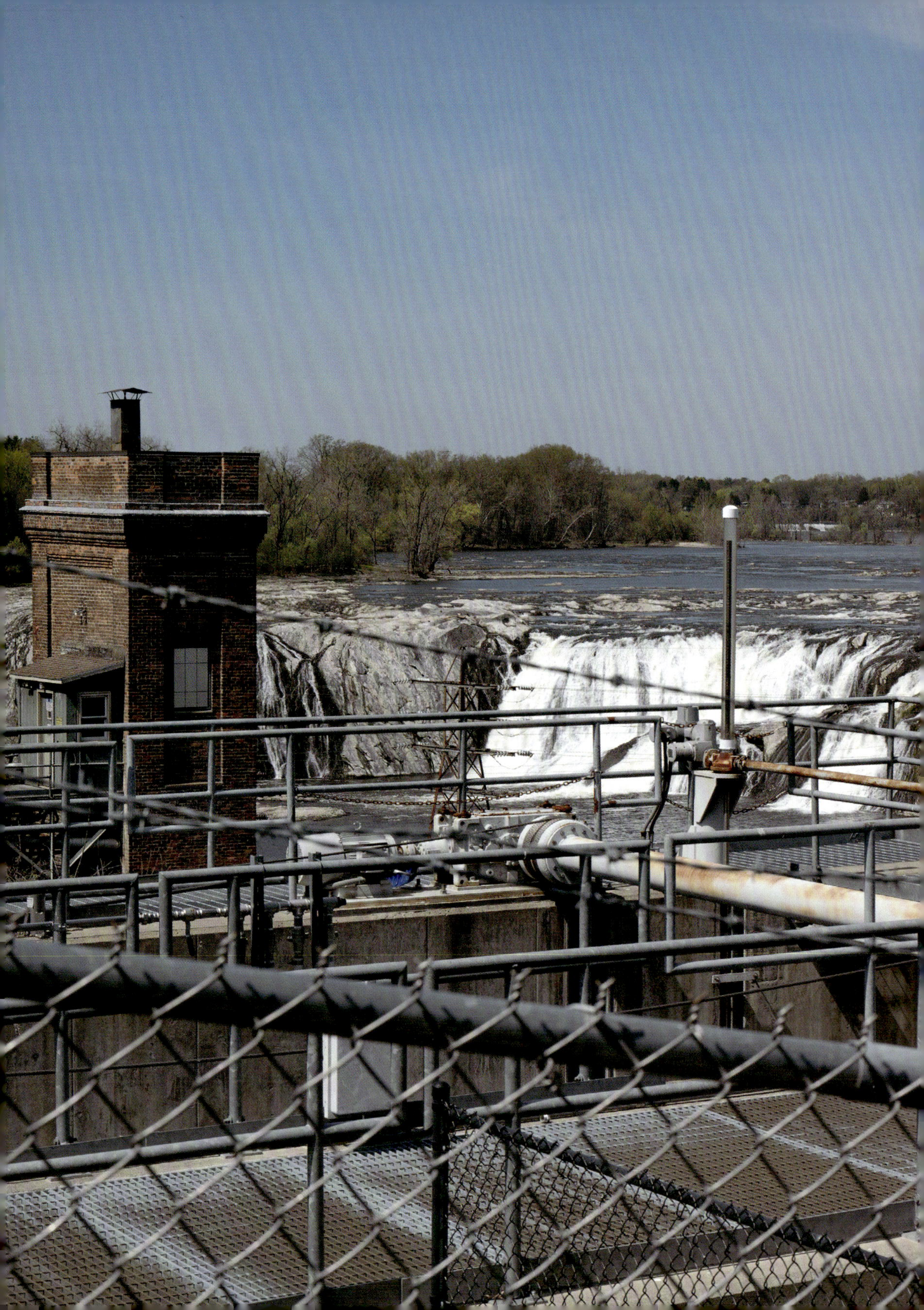

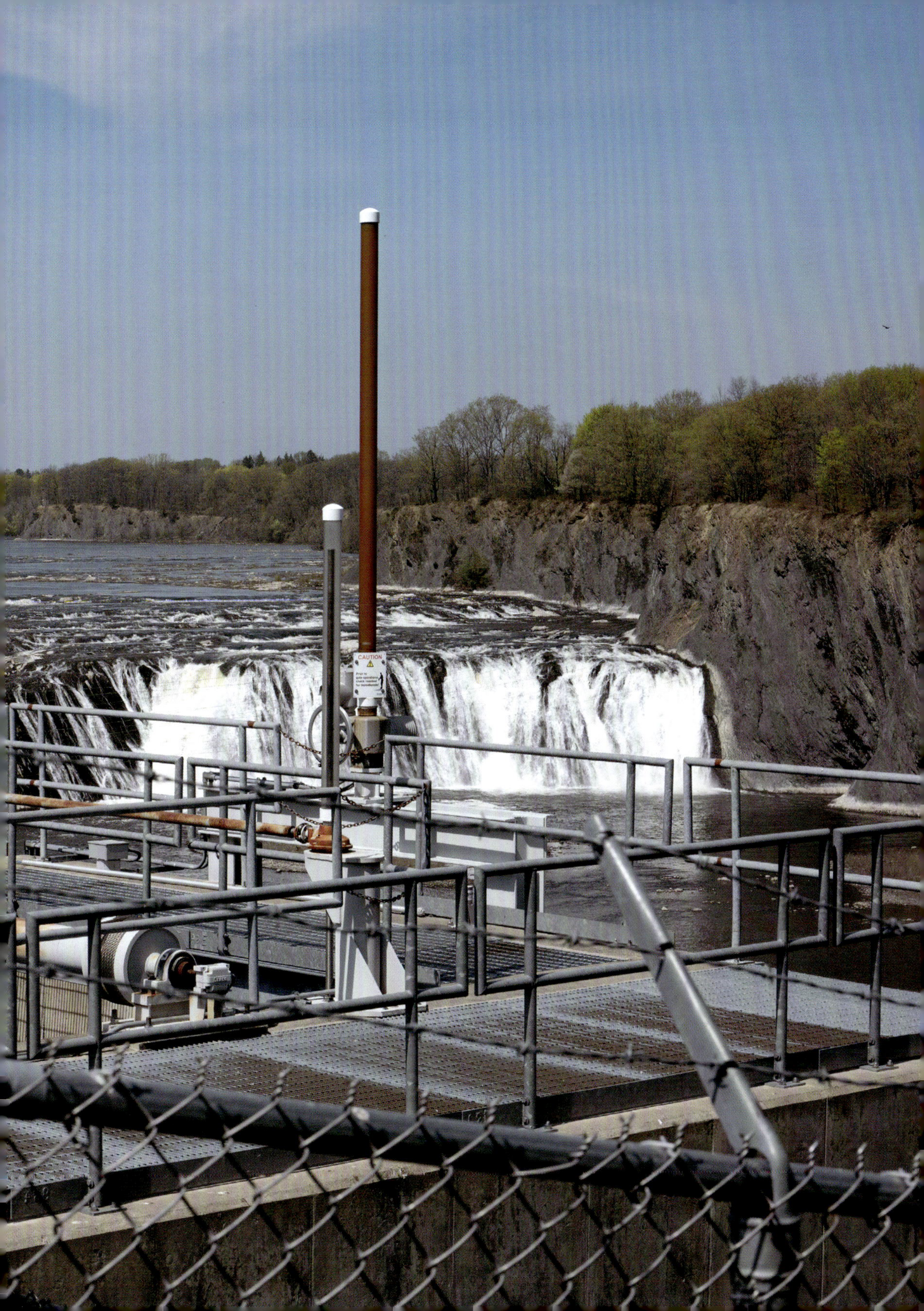
CAUTION

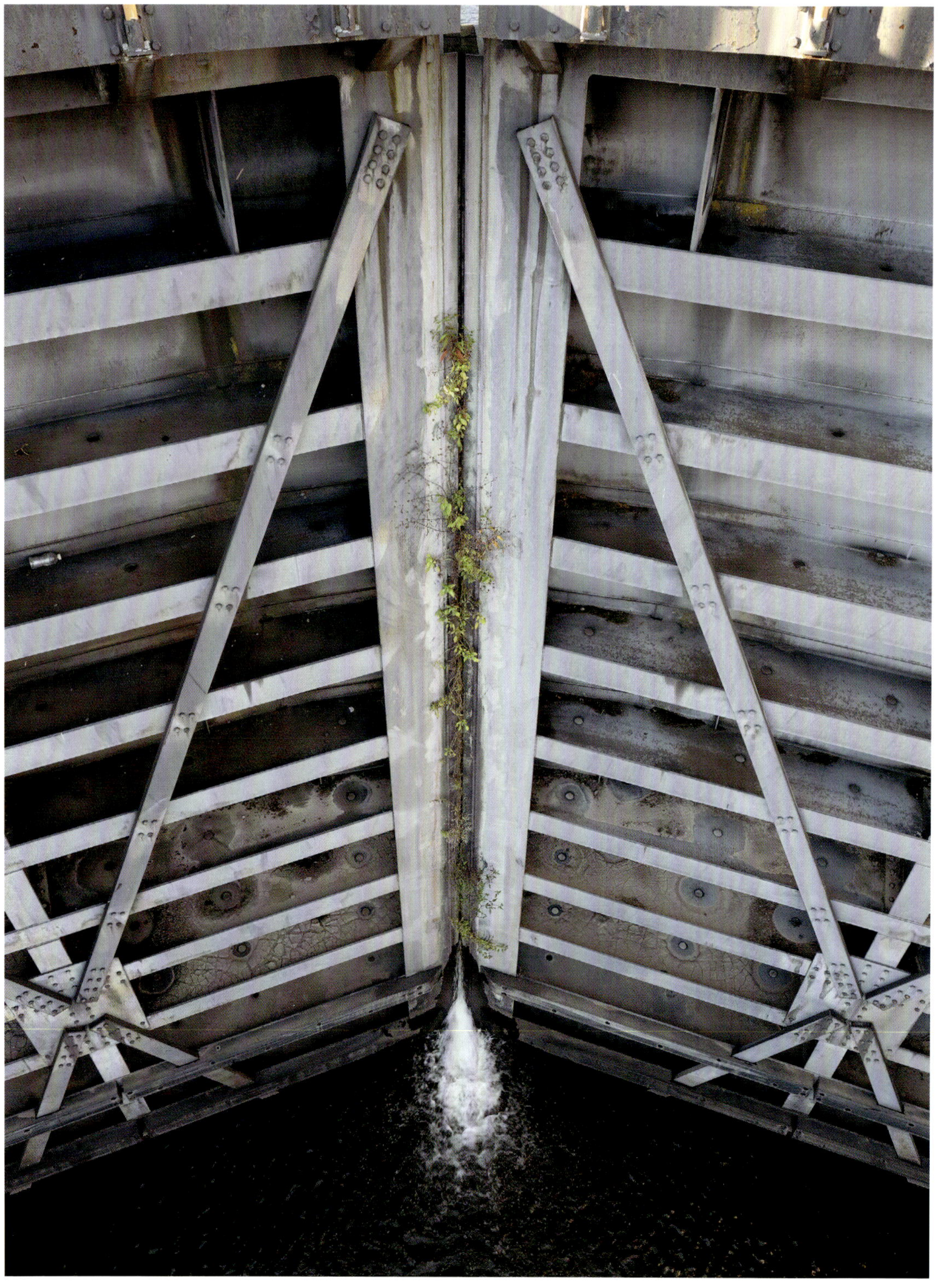

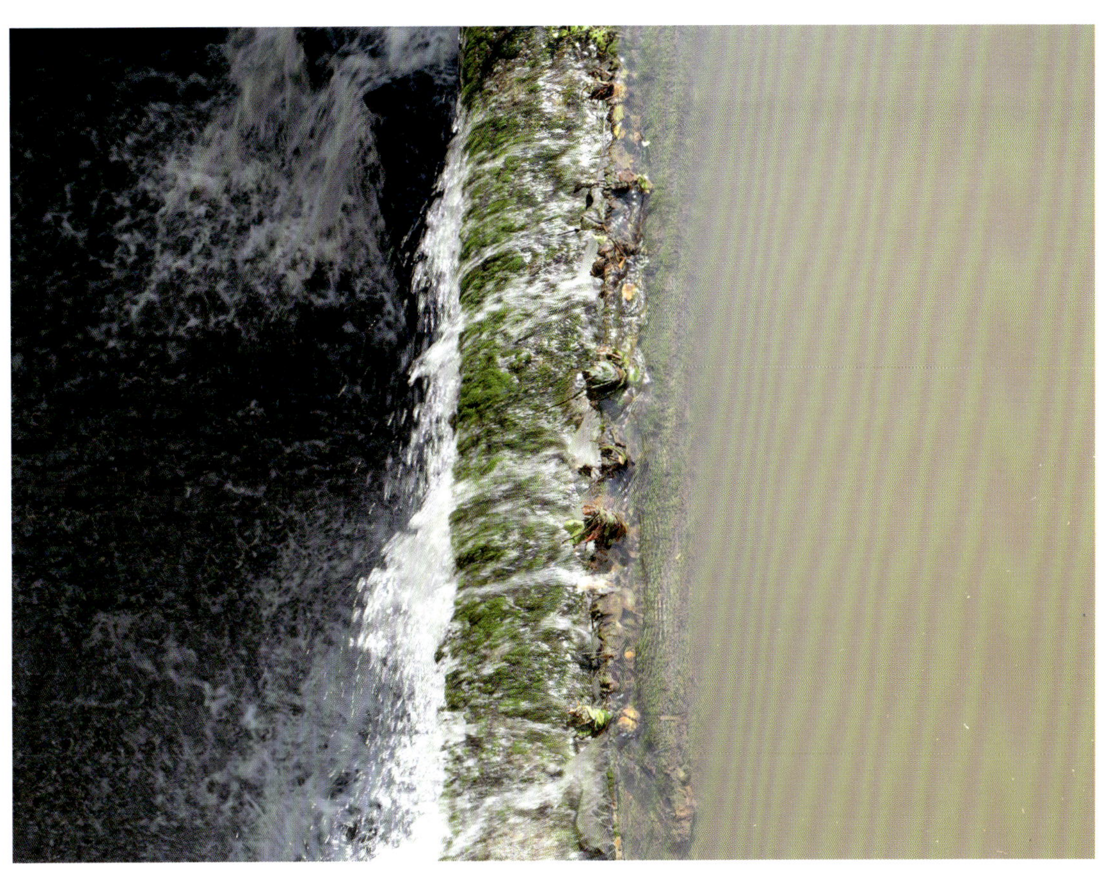

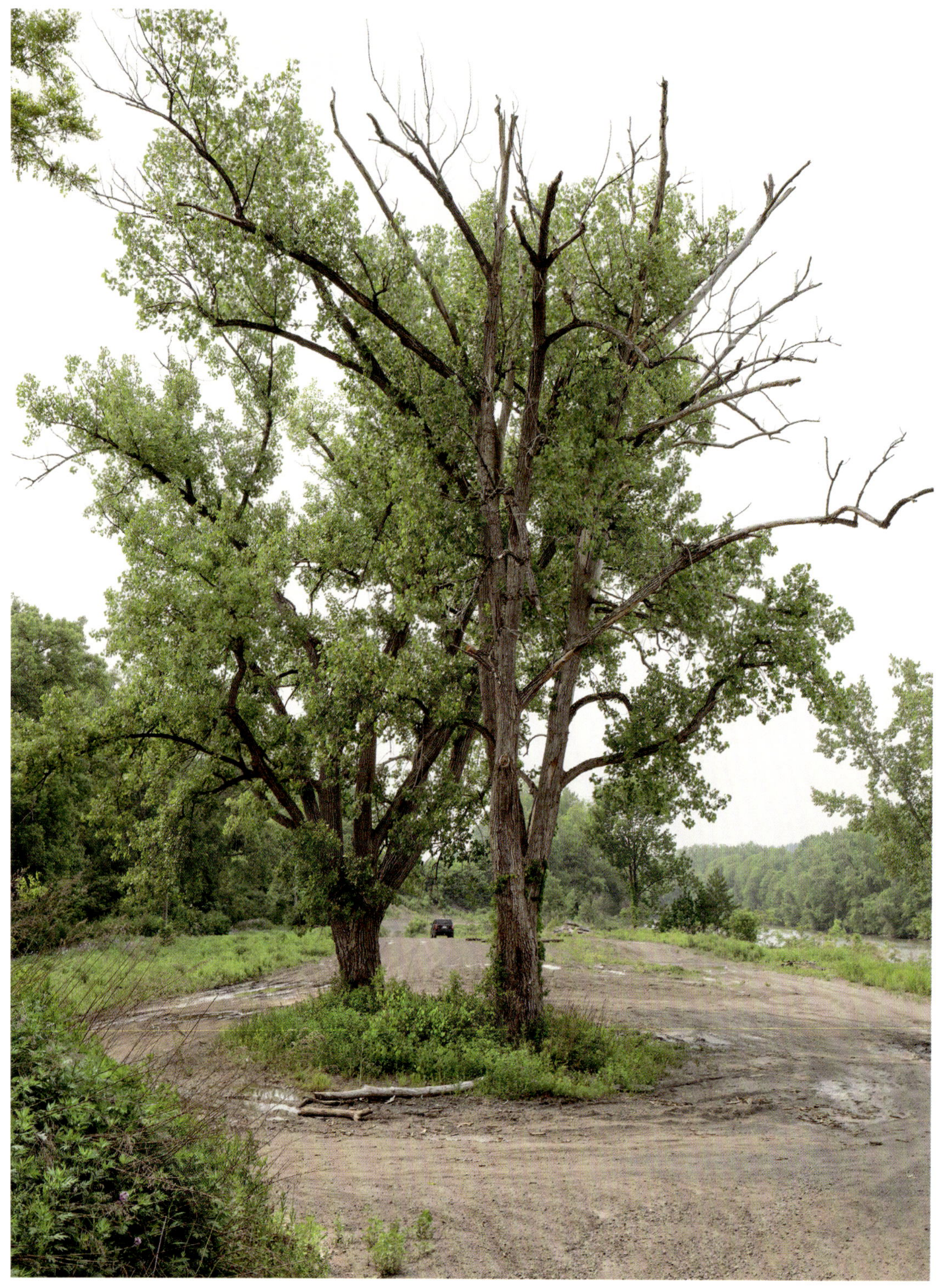

I work In The Levees during the Winter. I deal with Cold temps. and Slippery Conditions while running Heavy Equipment sometimes on High Levee Banks that are Narrow. It can also be difficult to Clean the tracks out at End of Each Day Due to the Dirt and Snow Freezing up

Alot of People Don't Understand
what a Dredge Boat Actual Does.
Or the process Involved in this
Job. Also Alot of Boaters
Don't understand the need to
Contact A working Vessel Before
going by us.

The Most Challenging
task I face is Working
Hastily with Weather
Conditions and Time
Restrictions We face in
A Short Maintenance
Season in Section 8.
Conditions Can be dangerous
@ Locks and unpredictable
Depending on snow,
ice, and Time.

Answer phones
Data entry
Time entry
Payroll entry
run reports for payroll
SAP / CATS
Onboarding employees
problem Assist with/for employees
Process/submit for boot reimbursements
Travel voucher reimbursements
Submit invoices through Process director
Log hours of labor into Maximo

Process PO's/requisitions
putting out 'Small fires' daily.
Injury reports

HRAA filed in HC
Track job postings
fill out probationary reports

PLANNING TASKS THAT NEED
TO BE DONE IN A TIMELY
MANNER AND TO HAVE EQUIPMENT
BACK TOGETHER AND FUNCTIONING
FOR THE NEXT NAVIGATION SEASON

PLANNING TASKS THAT NEED
TO BE DONE IN A TIMELY
MANNER AND TO HAVE EQUIPMENT

DEGREASING

GEARS

Saving animels from The
Lock chamber That Accidently
— Fell in. l saveD A Boston Terrior
From The Lock chamber at 28-A
Last season.

        Clearing Ice
— Shoveling wellcways keeping
Areas Safe. — pulling motors

AnD electrical Componets

      keeping equipment (Greased)
    — AnD ReaDy for
      The next season

I think the whole process of communication between the different locks is something that is way more involved than someone outside of the canals would assume - lock keepers, and to some extent, boaters, are always on the phone/radio to each other to coordinate and make travel as seamless as possible for everyone involved.

The day started for me
the night before the flood
I was night man water control
the water came up so
fast at Lock 18 that was
trapped at lock with car
being swamped. The Grade
14 Came in at got me
Out with a ten wheel track
Wow what a day!

Many folks don't understand how our Locks work. Most people think we pump water back and forth when in reality we don't pump any water to operate Locks. They are all gravity-fed.

Non-new season involves a lot of rehab work at our pump out site. Also, most of our vessels return to the section HQ and go into dry dock. There is a lot of planning that goes into all that work. That becomes a challenge.

Alot of people think we
All work on the locks.
Then we'll tell them that we
do buoy setting And picking, we
pick debris (trees And other things) from
Canal, we dredge, most people have
no idea.

I am A welder and ReHab
VAlve's for the Lock's 4
valve's per Lock and it
Keep's me Busey its we Do
All The VAlve's From waterford
To FoRt EdwARd.
and The EIRE caNAl's FoNdA
and All The Other sectioNs
out west.

During non-Nav. season,
floating plant crews work on
maintainance on vessels. We all help
each other. Some crews will
work in a U.D.S. (upland disposals, too)
working to restructure the site and
make ready for an upcoming
digging season, including putting in
spill boxes, restructuring fingers,
building up walls etc. We use
bulldozers, excavators, Bobcats,
whatever is necessary.

The ANNUAL rebuilding of
Lock Equipment which includes:
unwiring & unbolting the motors,
Limit Switches, control boards and
resistor grids. The Equipment is manually
removed by the "over the Hill gang" and
placed in the workshop. We also assist
other Locks with their Equipment.
Once the Equipment has been removed,
the disassembly of the motors, boards, Limit
+over travel Switches and grids can begin.
The Equipment is broken down to the
smallest component and painted, polished,
deburred, revarnished and rebuilt.
In some cases, parts have to be remanufactured
or something newer modified. All so Everything
can work as intended.

In the Fall we Remove
Heavy electrical equipment from
cabinets. We move it to our
onsite work shop where we
disassemble inspect and Refinish it
Before Reassembly. Then Reinstalled
in cabinets Before Navigation
Season.

Most people think we just
sit and wait for boats. They're
surprised when I tell them that
the person running the lock, paints
the lock, greases the equipment, mows the
lawn, answers the phone + questions, gives
a "tour" of the lock, historical talks
about the old/new canals. Some people
have asked me to help plan their trip
to the area. We also are a water
control structure, so I have to move my
sluice gates per the Hydrologist to control
a 17 mile pool between me and lock 32
in Pittsford. We also monitor rainfall,
snow surveys and report to the National
Weather Service. Last year we recieved our
100yr certificate from NWS.

Talking with boaters on where they can
find mooring and get a good meal is also
something we do

OPENING VALVES TO
ALLOW THE GATES TO OPEN.

H_2O IS EXTREMELY STRONG.

THE GATES WILL WAVER WHEN
THE H_2O HAS GOTTEN INTO
EQUILIBRIUM. VERY COOL.
SPECTATORS ARE VERY IMPRESSED.

Today is a double up day, so there's
two of us. Most of the time it's just me
and there's too many things to do in between
running the locks. And it just doesn't seem
safe, something happens to me, there's no
one around.

THE AMOUNT OF WORK
IT TAKES THAT GOES INTO
OPERATING AND MAINTAINING
THE OPERATIONAL READINESS
THATS REQUIRED. LACK OF
QUALIFIED HELP.

I work @ Court Street Damn... Regulating the water flow when needed to through the process of gates is a process that not many people would understand. I have always wanted to work on the canal since I was a kid. Mostly due to the rich history of the canal in NYS.

In 1825, when stone masons were done working the locks in Lockport, they began building cobblestone houses which i'm also a fan of. With easy access to the canal, farmers businesses flourished and it is an <u>honor</u> to work on the canal because of all of this local history. Thank you for the opportunity!

Vessel maintenance. Various items to attend to divided among two Tenders, 1 Push boat, 1 conventional Tug and a Hydraulic Dredge. Preventative maintenance/ inspections of all the above.

UDS/levee grading/maintenance- Prepping for the next navigation Season.

Biggest challenge is fitting/ completing all task in about five months, safely and properly.

The most challenging part of the non-nav season, for me at least, is the whole "pump-out" process. I was only really involved during the winter of 2021, but it's a lot of standing around in the cold, especially if you're a smaller, less experienced canal-er like I am/was. I can't lift much, don't have any kind of heavy equipment certifications or welding experience... Lots of waiting to hand other people whatever tools they need, and in my case - a fair amount of fitting into small spaces that no one else can reach. Hard work, but absolutely fascinating.

The reason we do tree Maintenance is not just for Looks. It Prevents dam. Failures and Blockeges important for water Level control

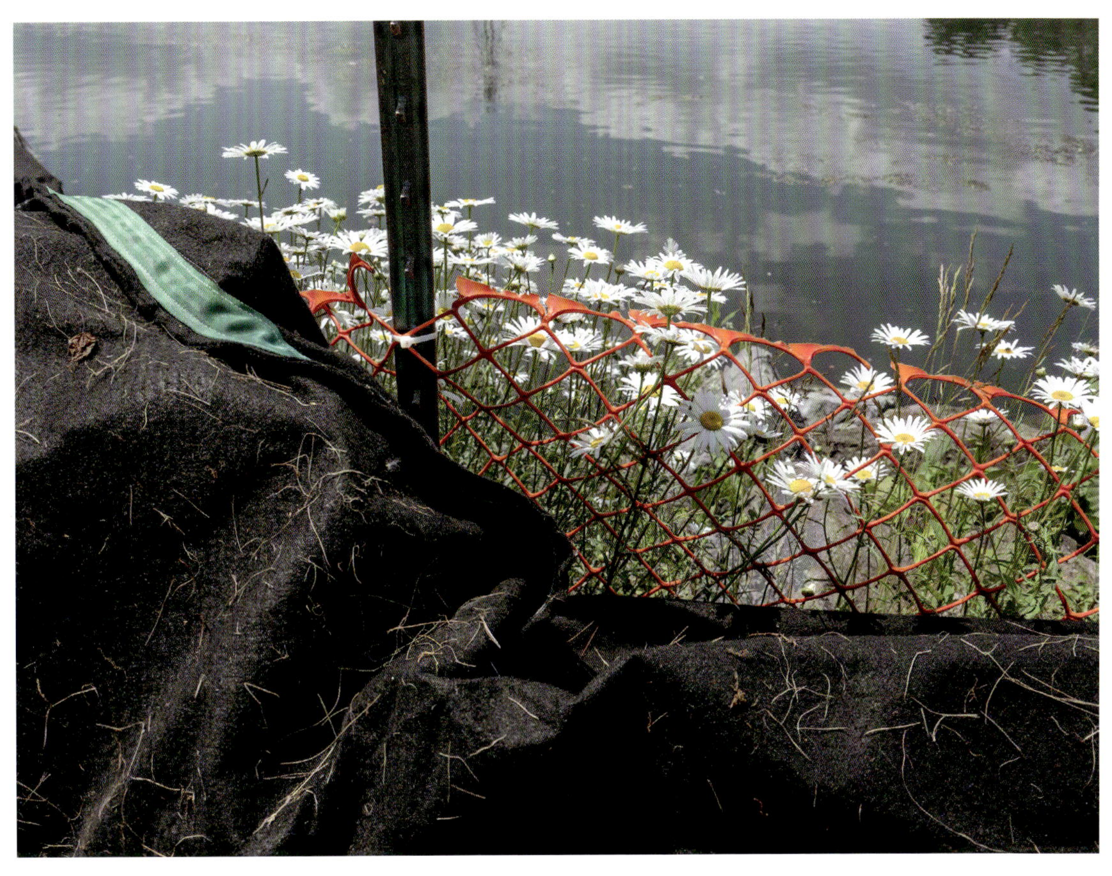

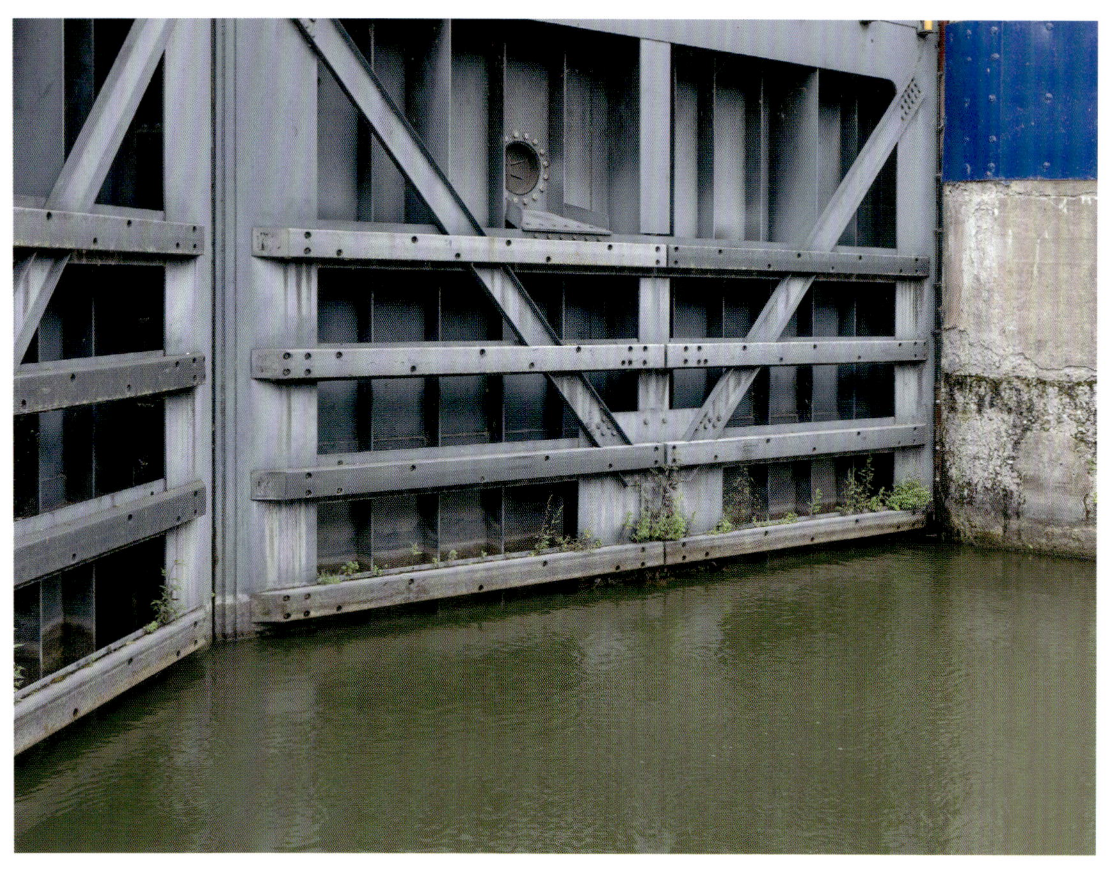

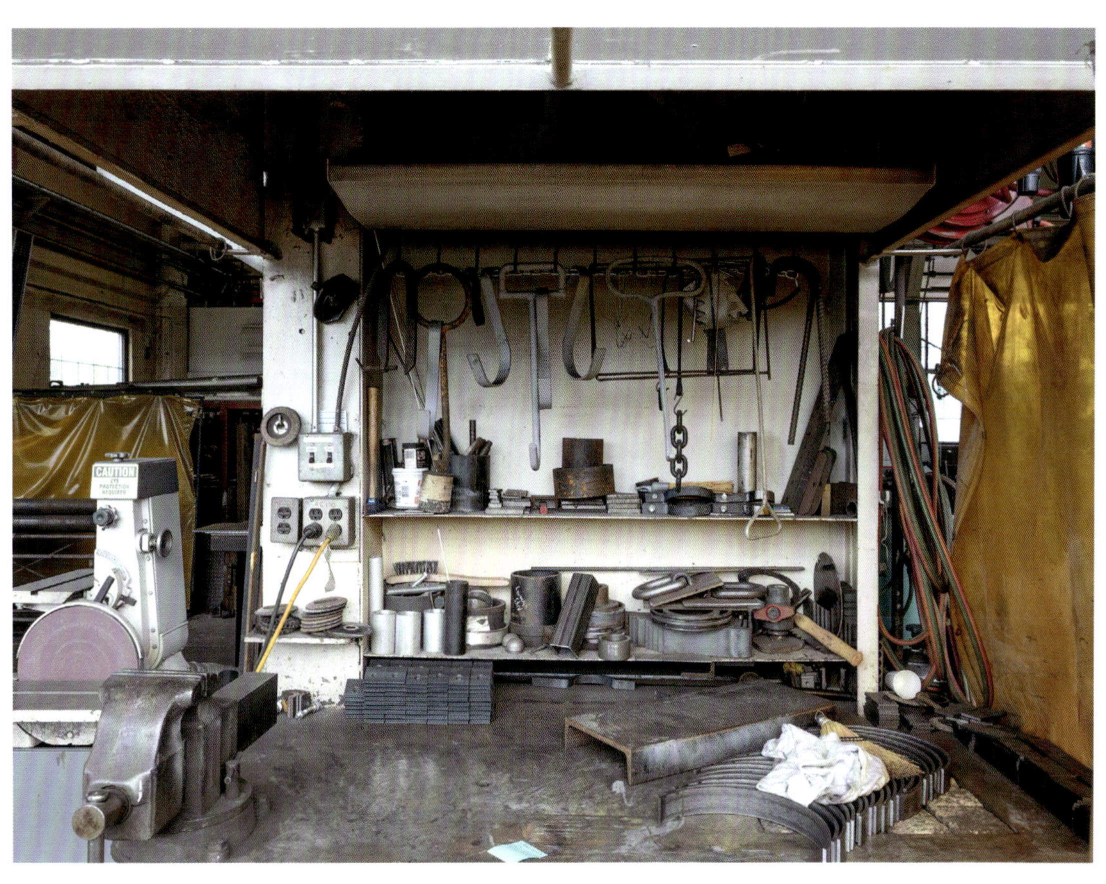

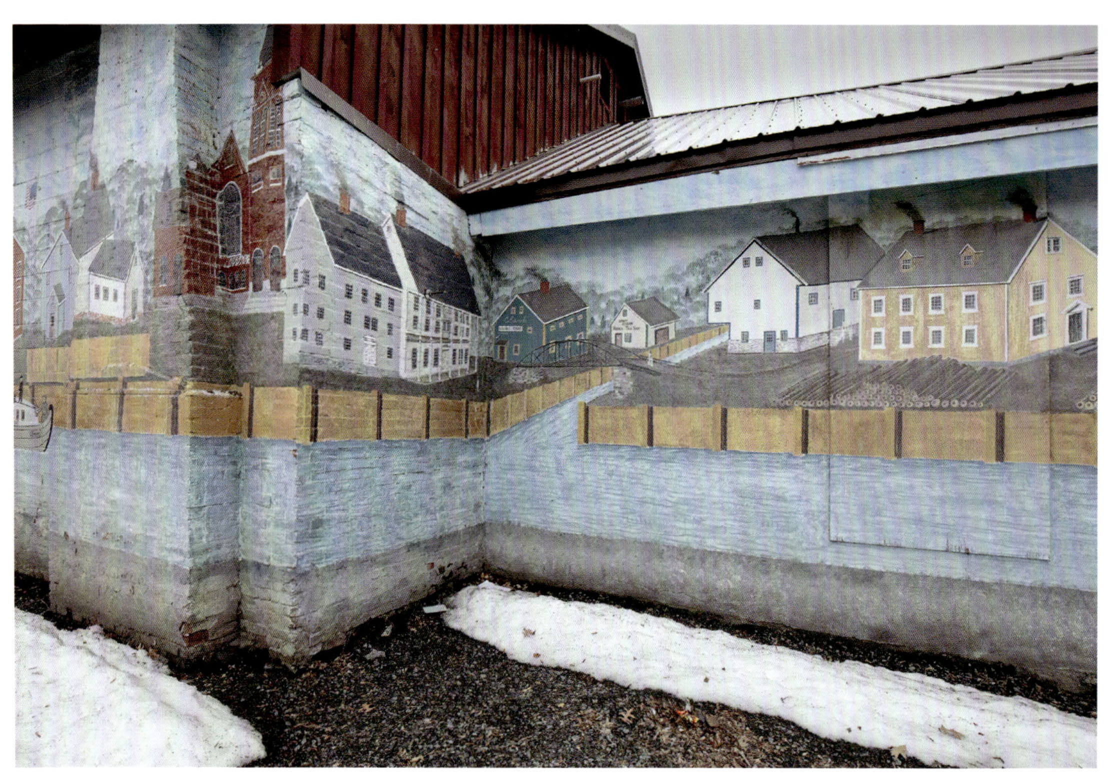

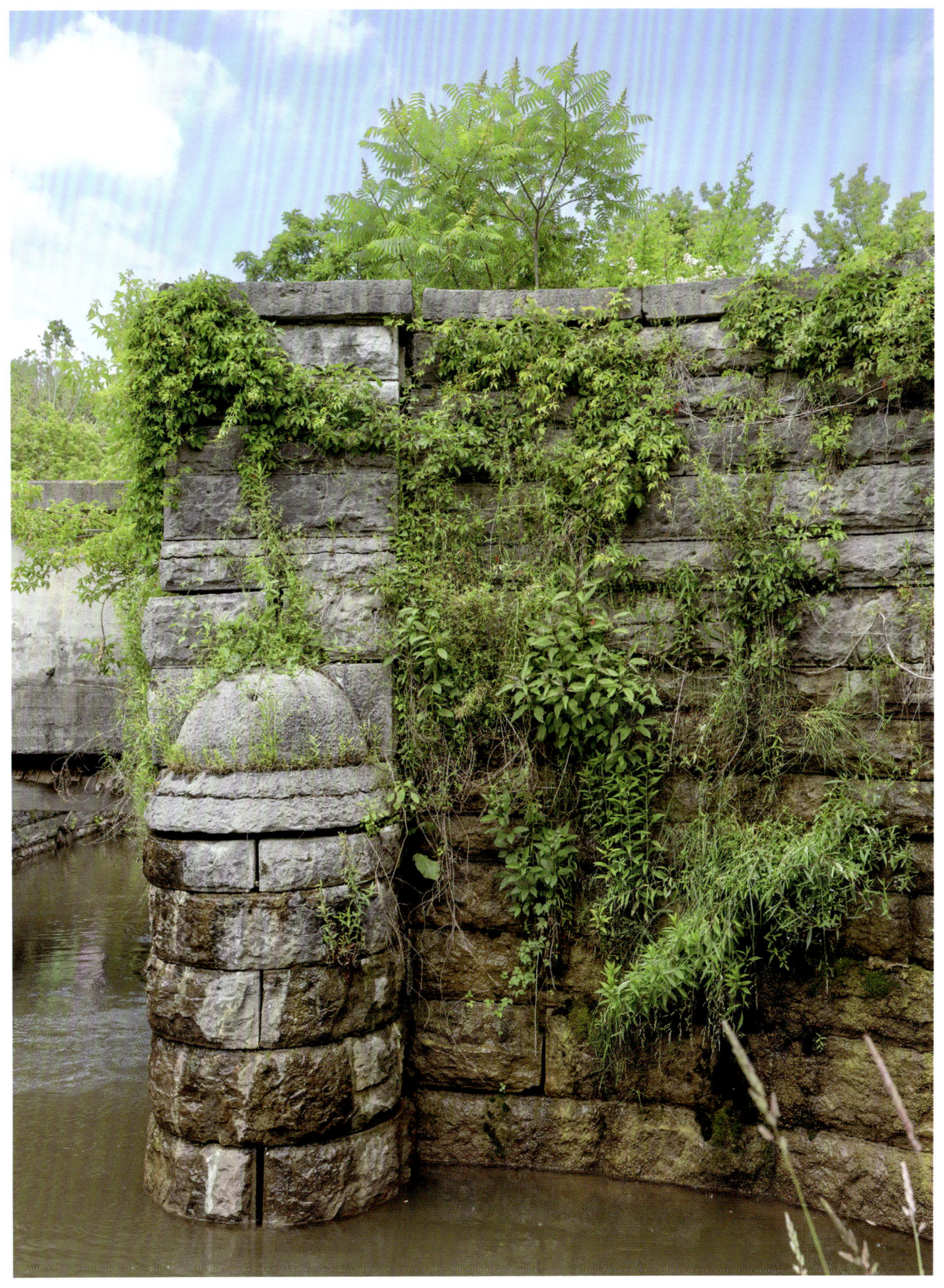

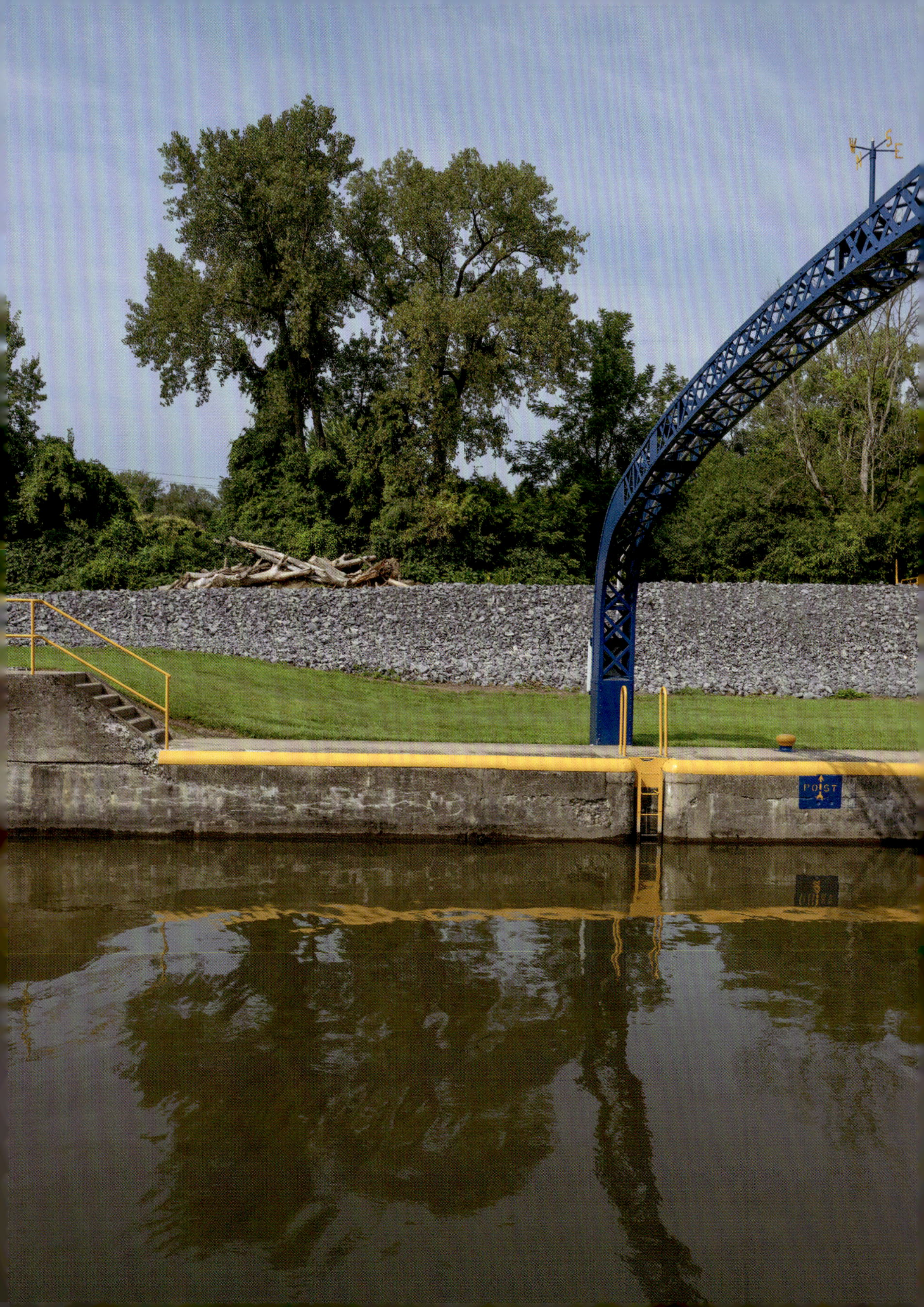

POST

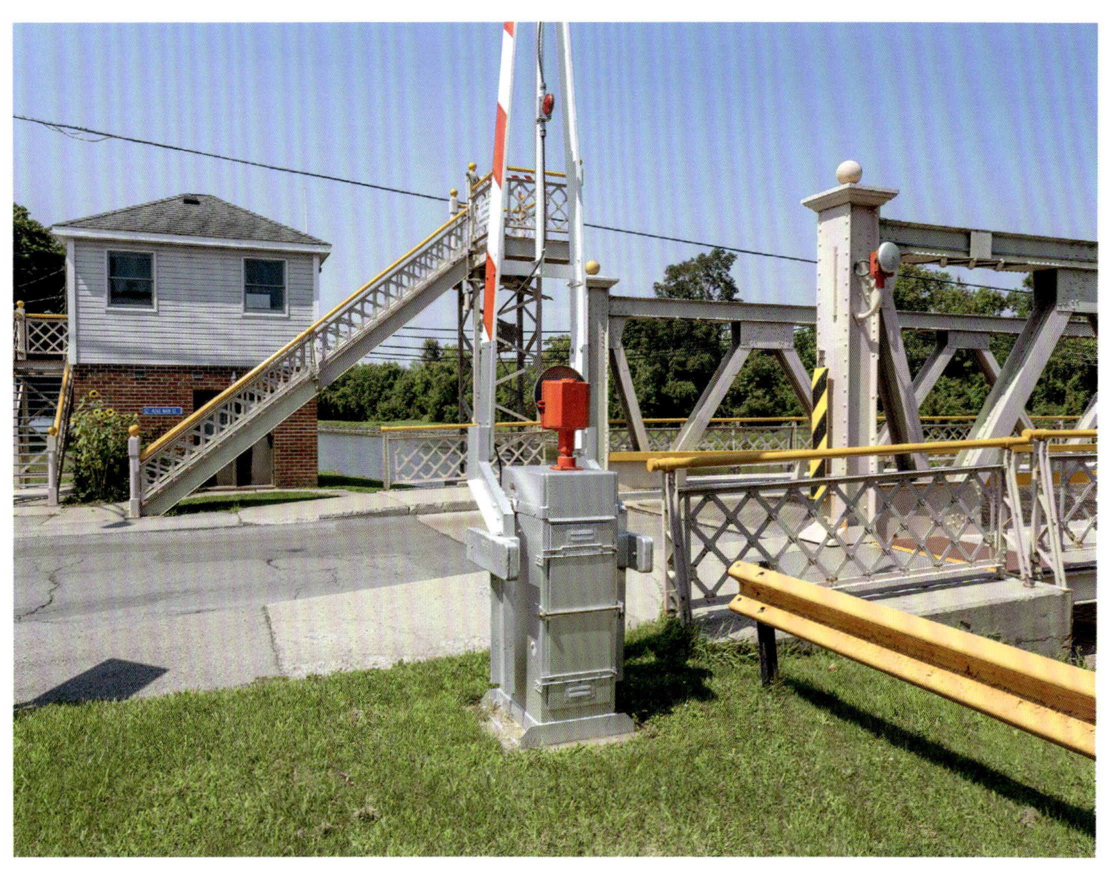

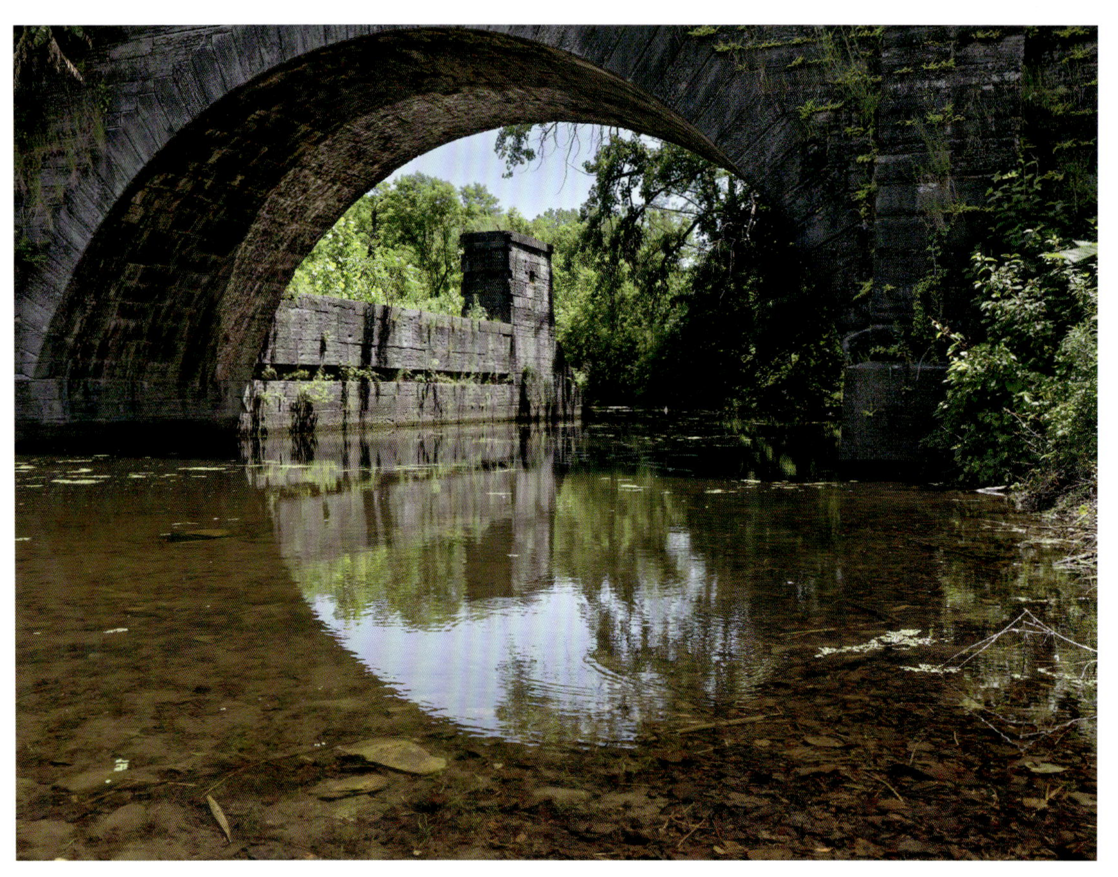

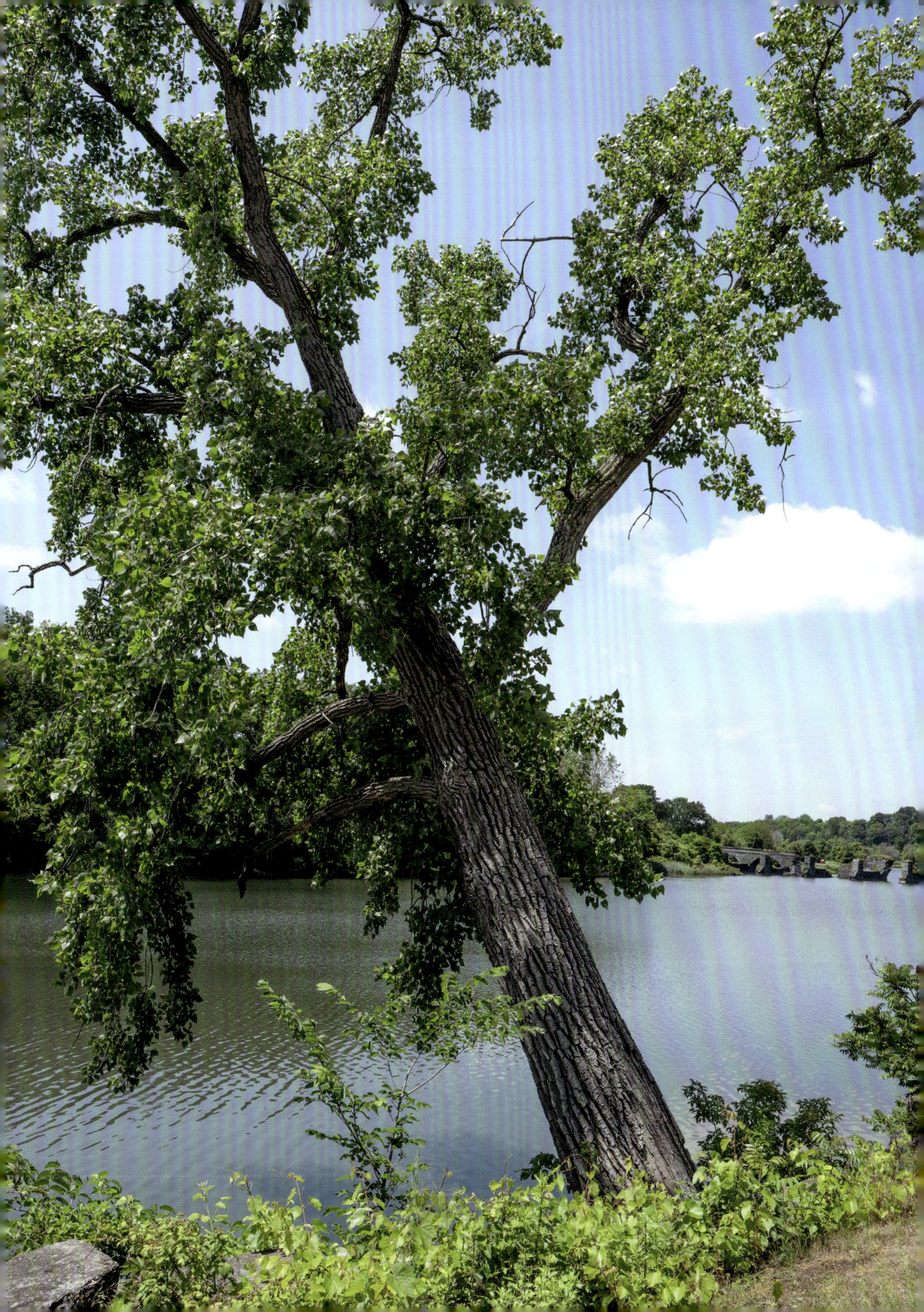

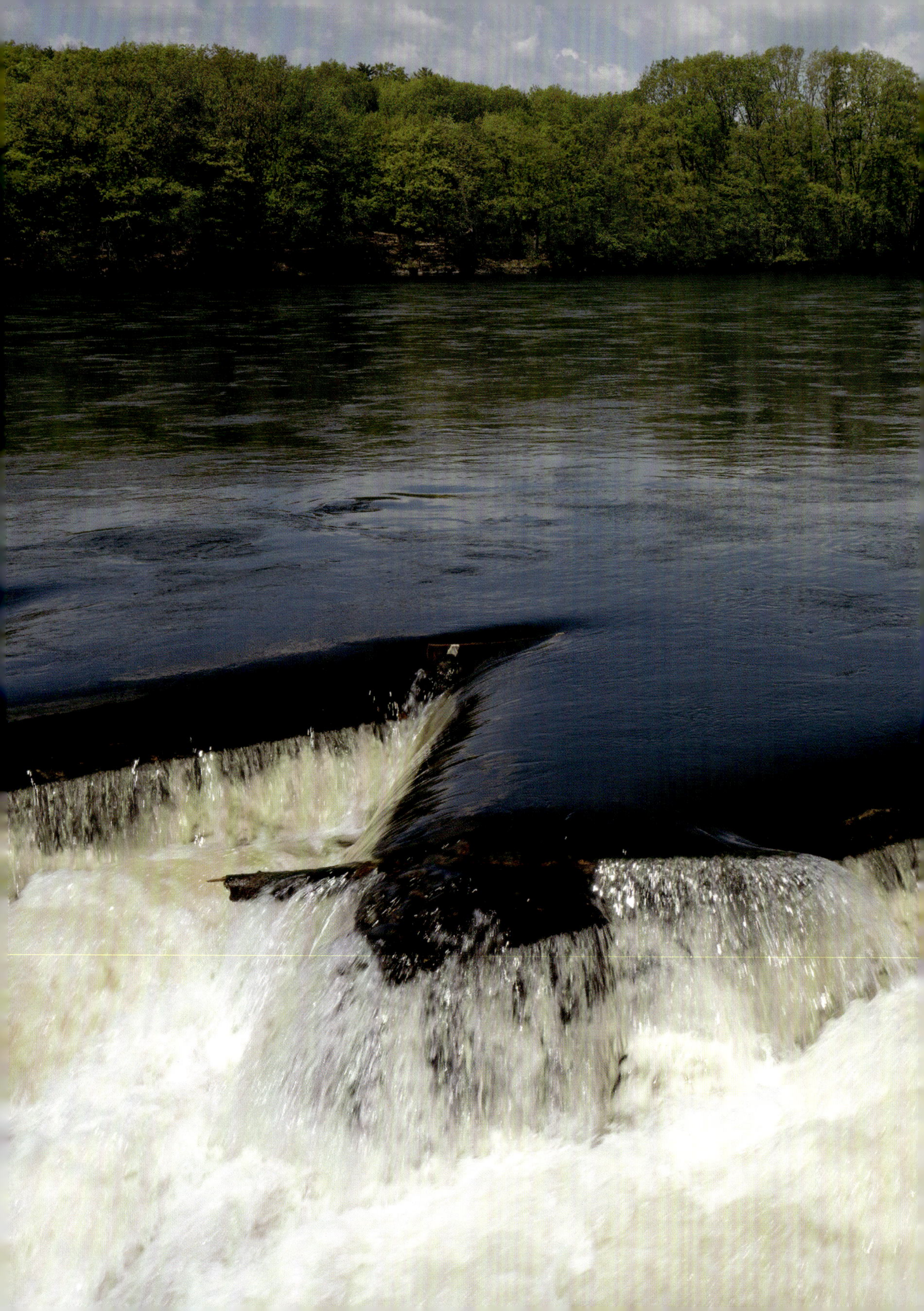

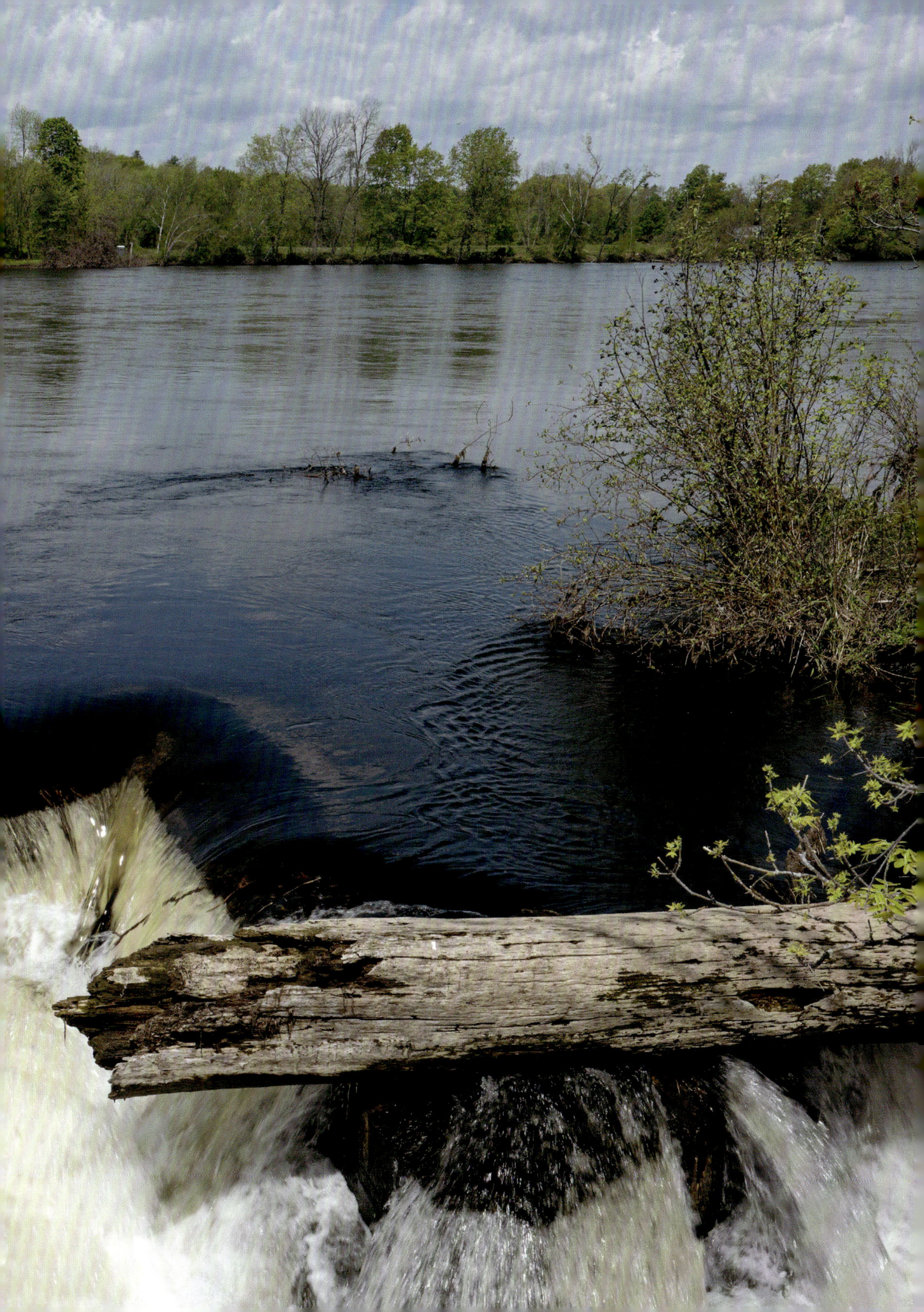

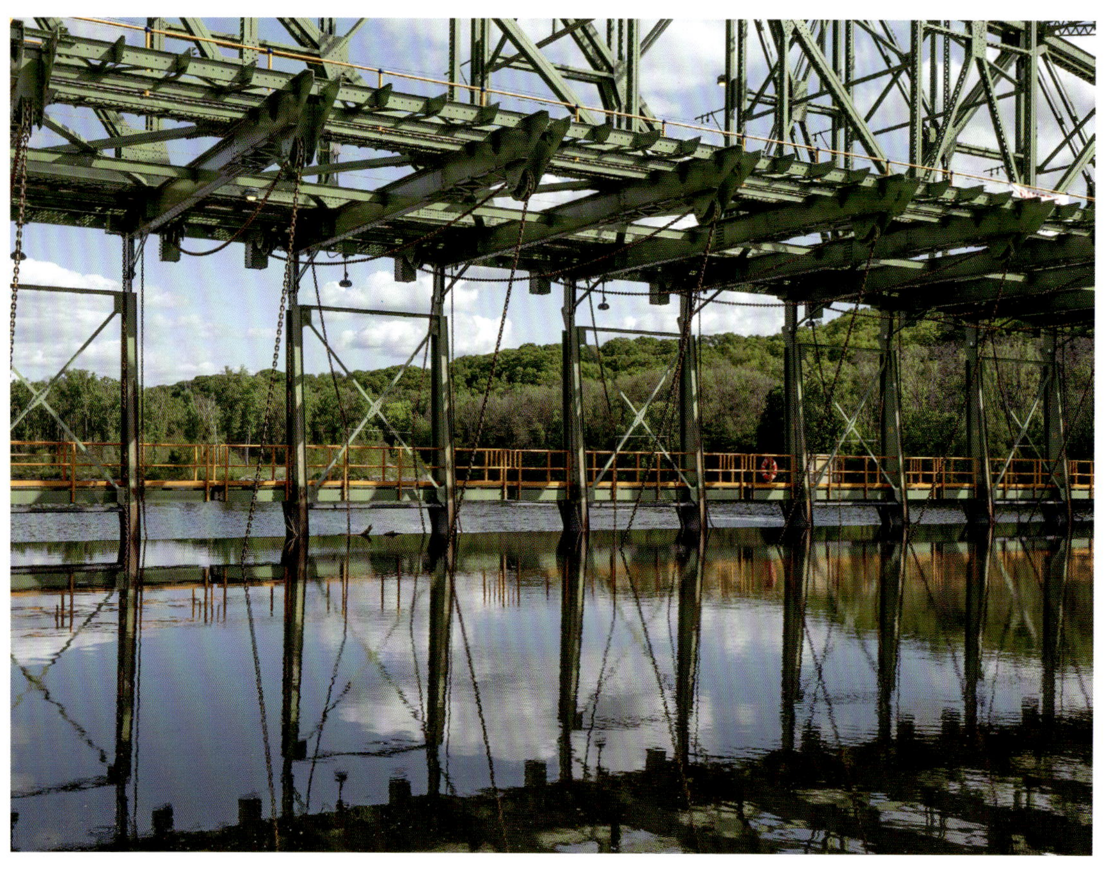

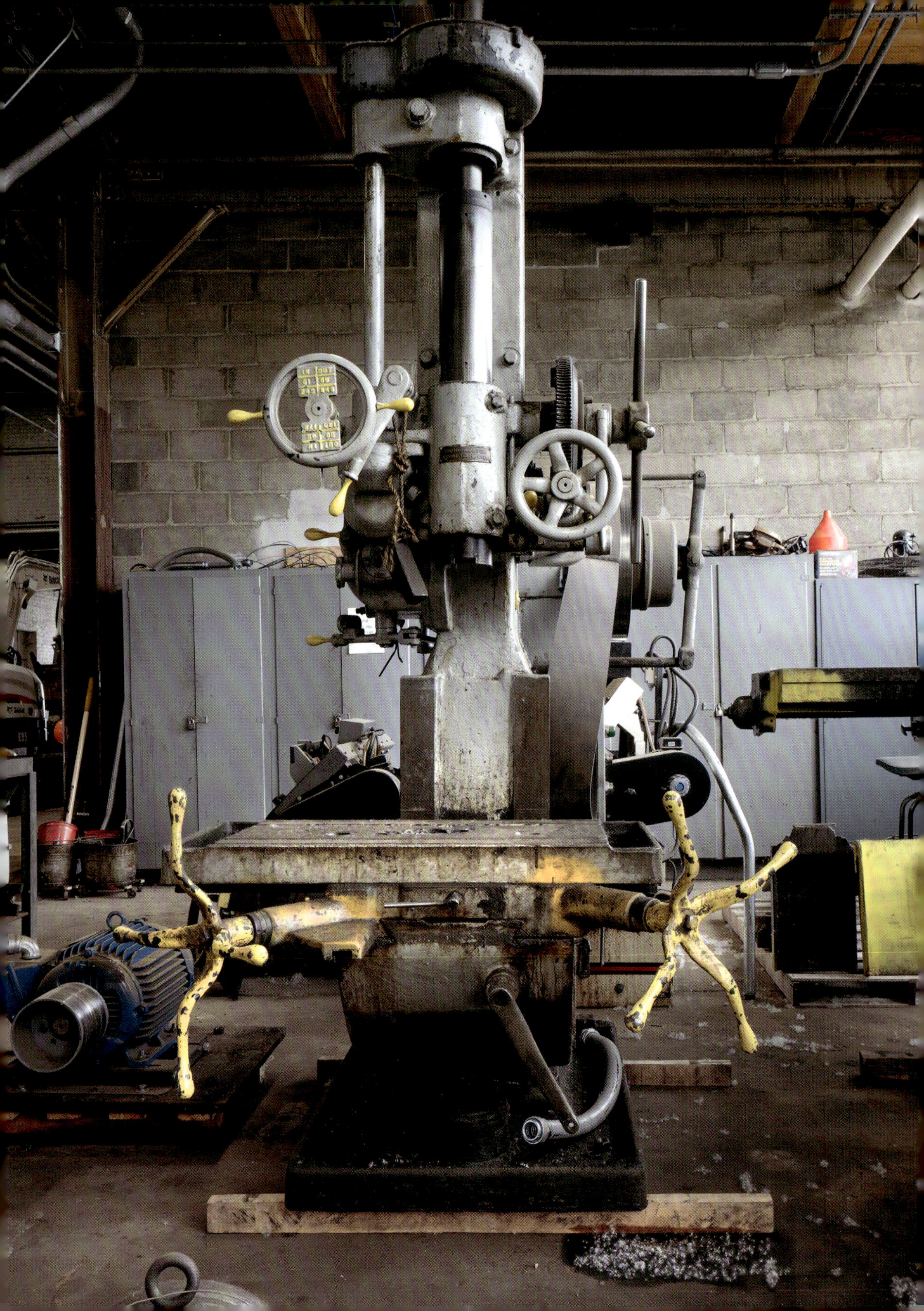

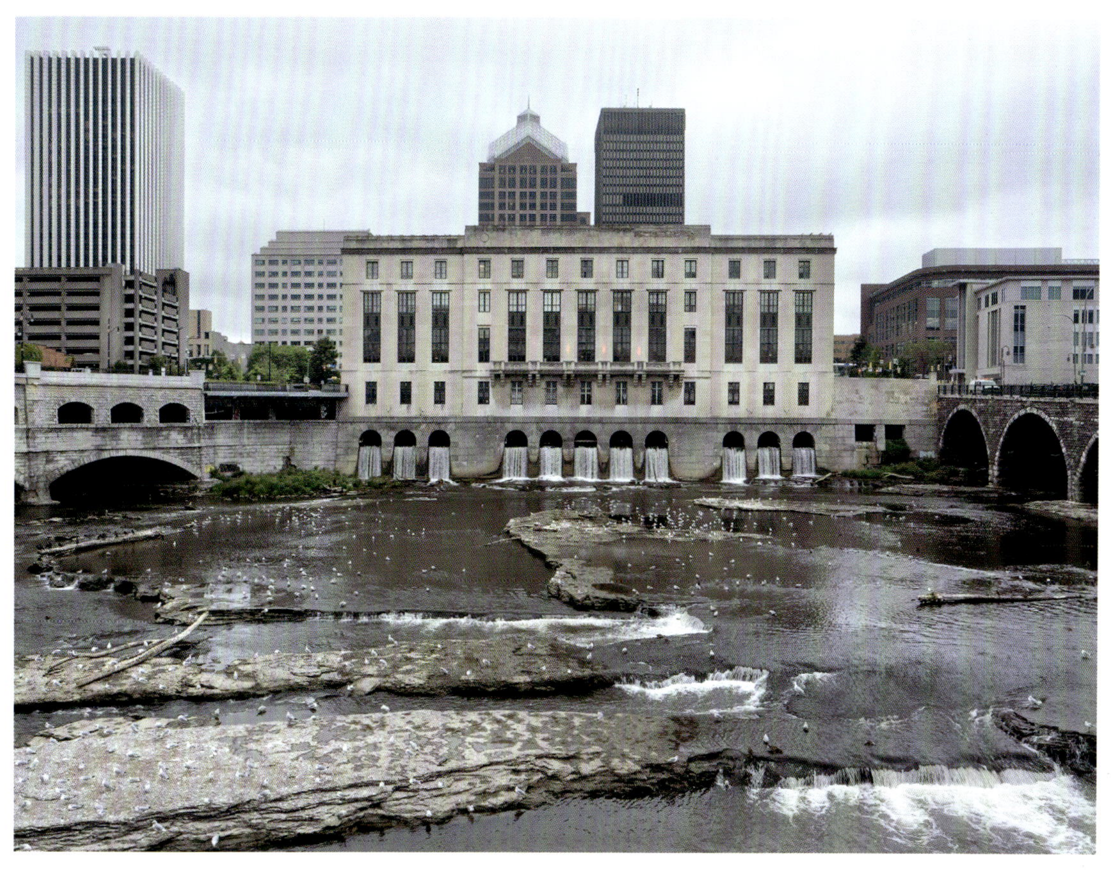

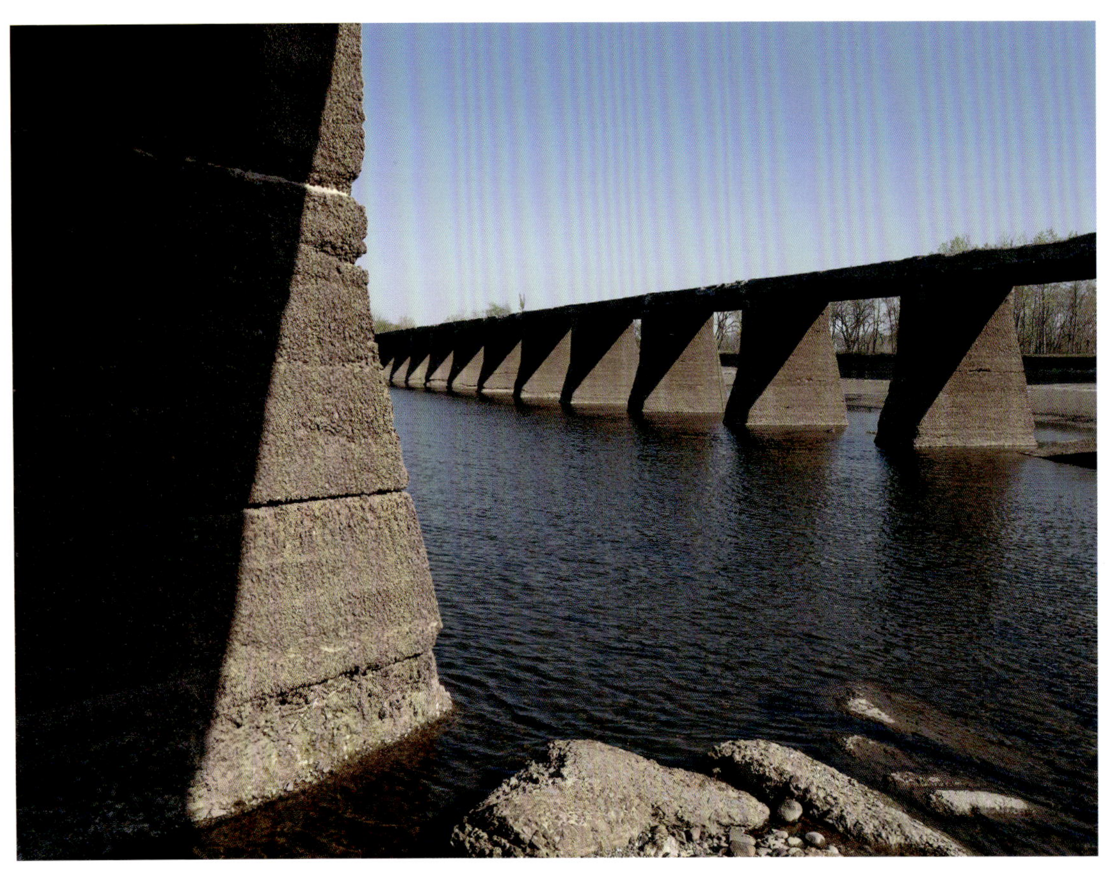

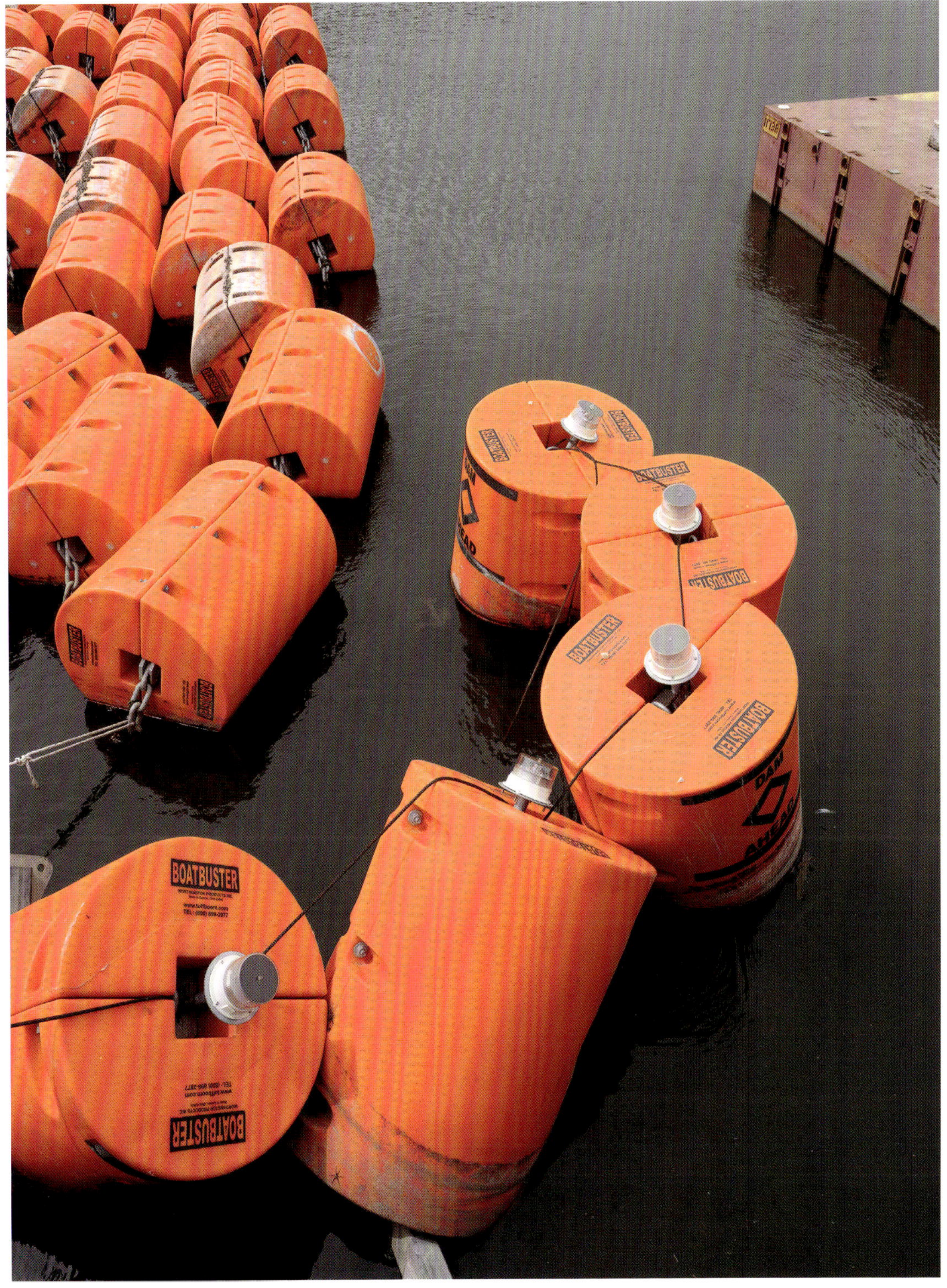

BOATBUSTER
BOATBUSTER
BOATBUSTER
BOATBUSTER
BOATBUSTER
DANGER
AHEAD
DAM
AHEAD
www.tuffboom.com
TEL: (800) 899-2877

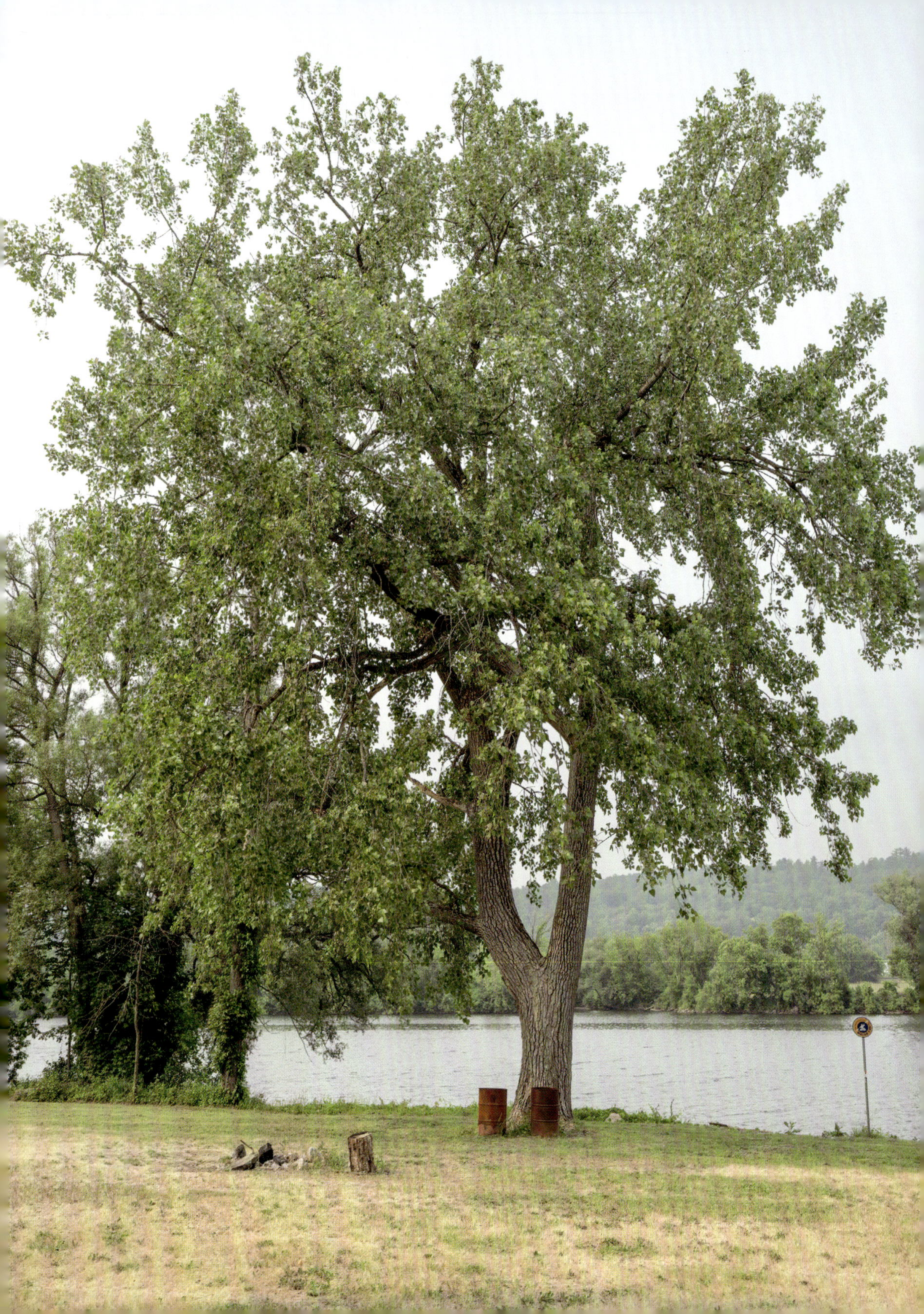

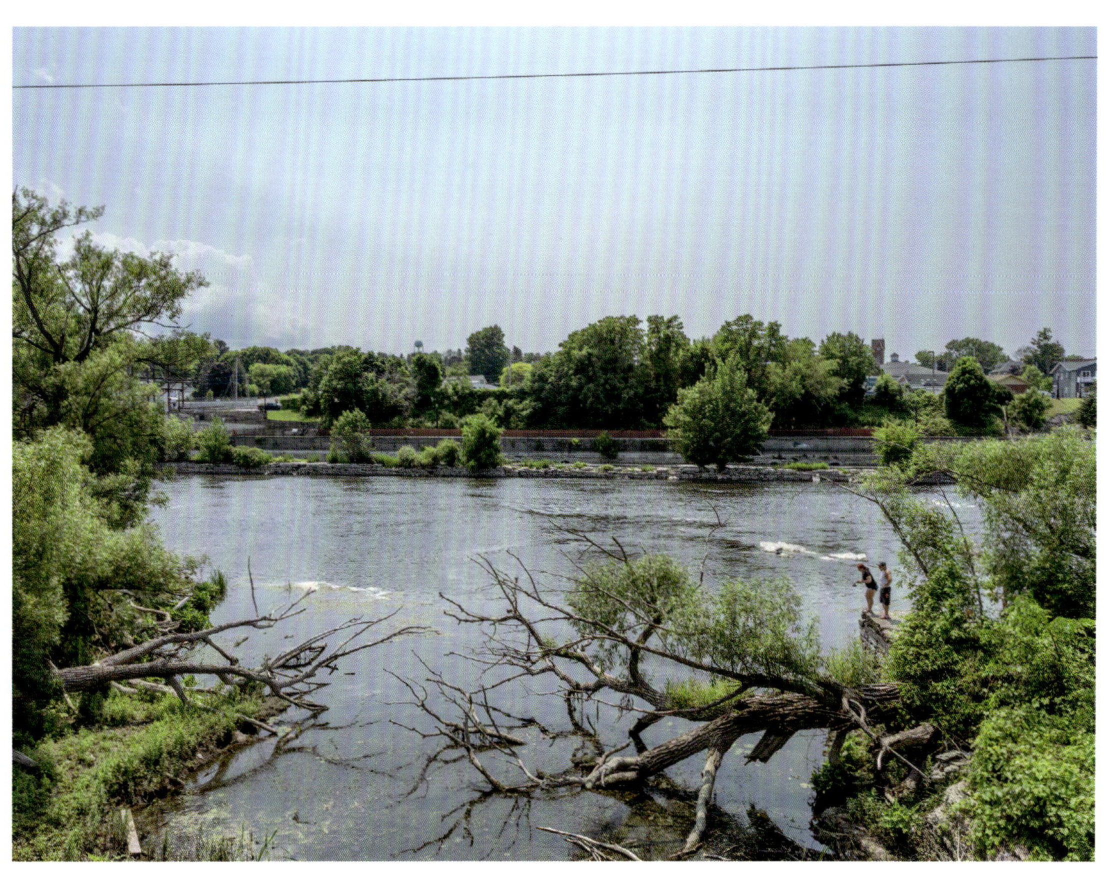

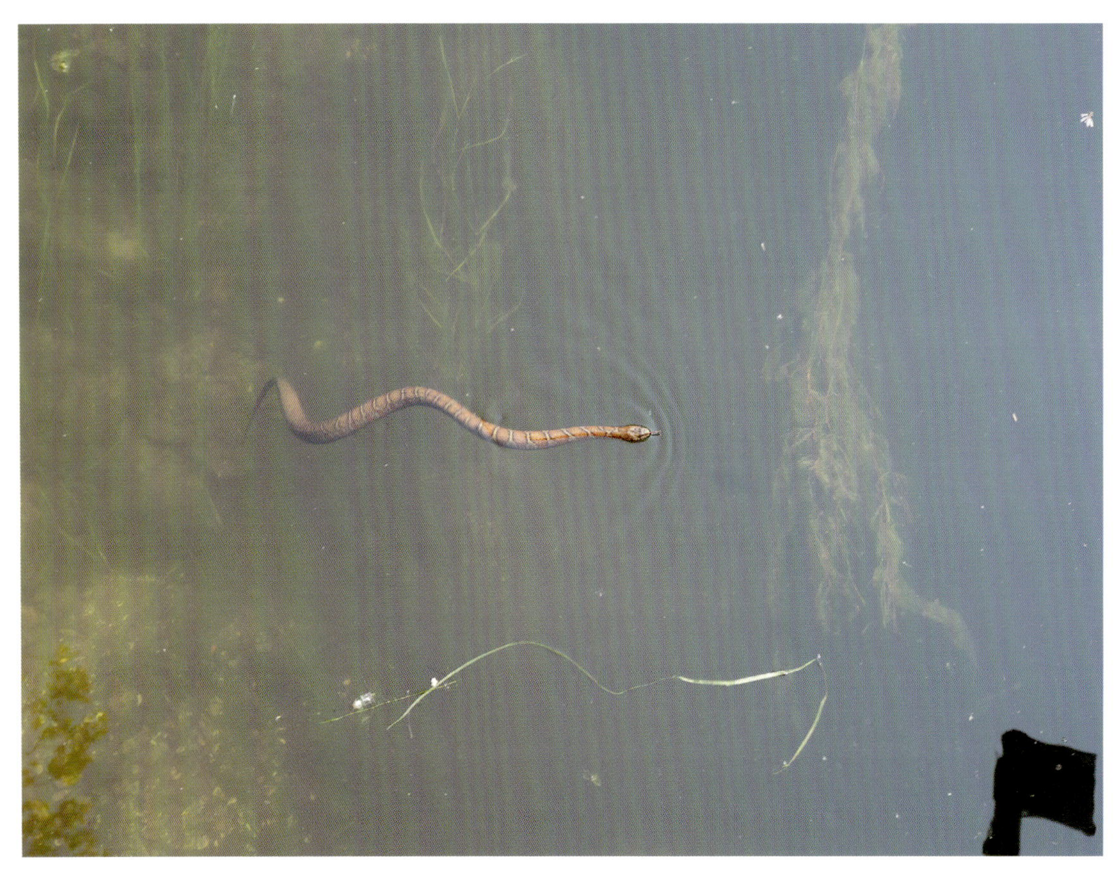

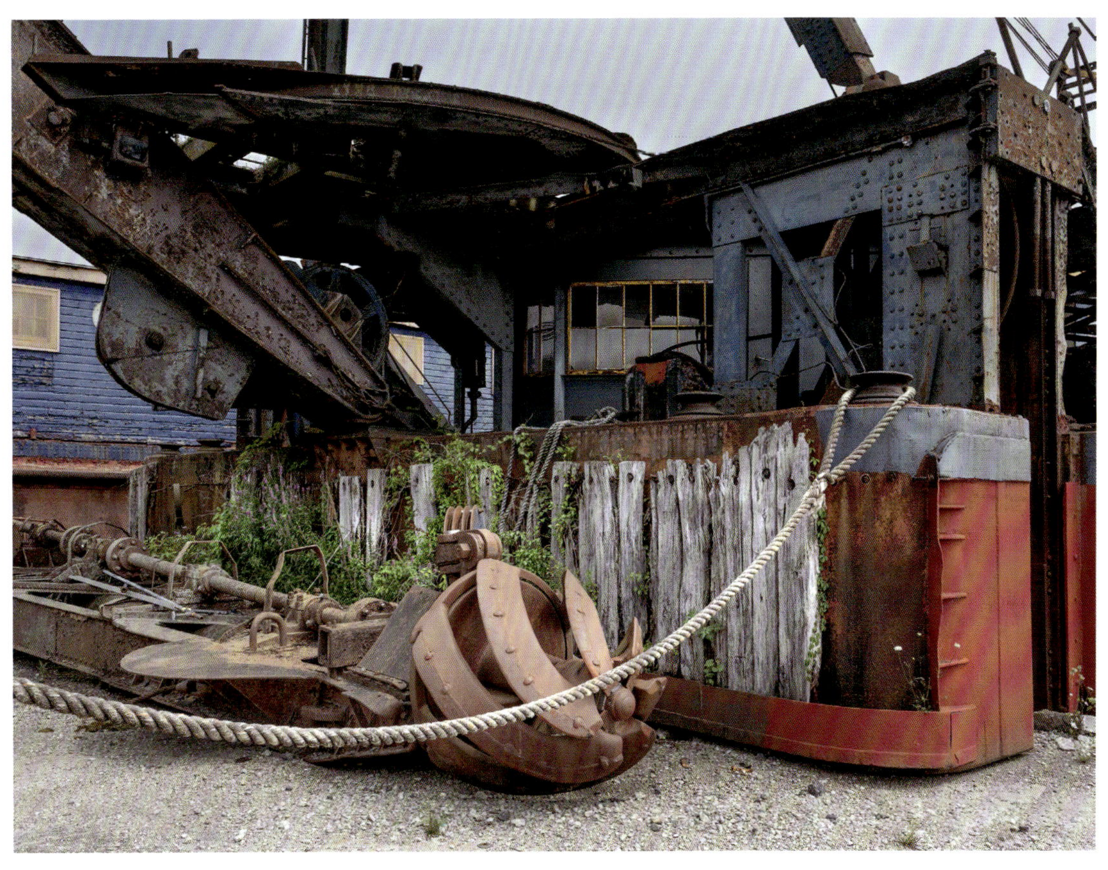

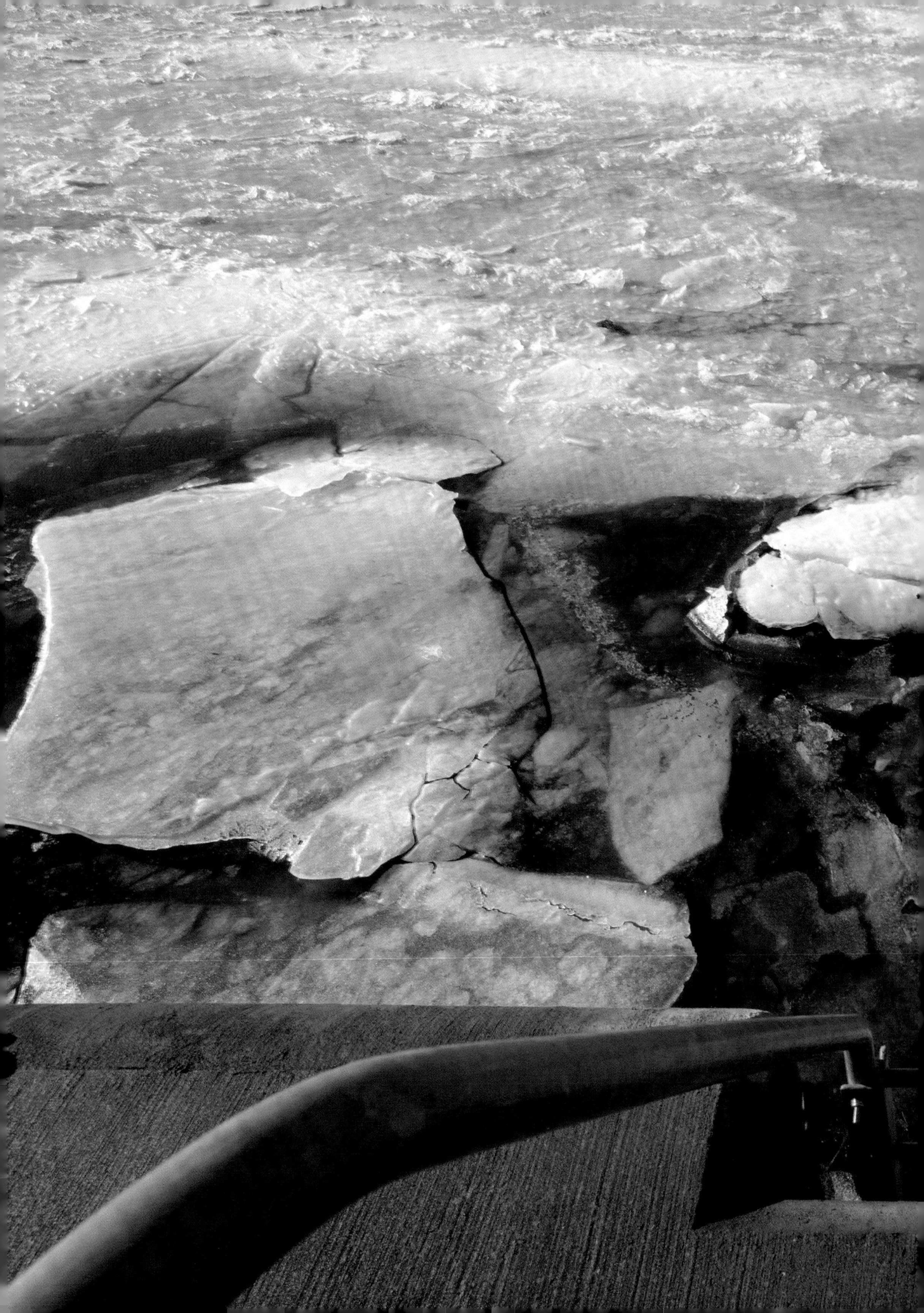

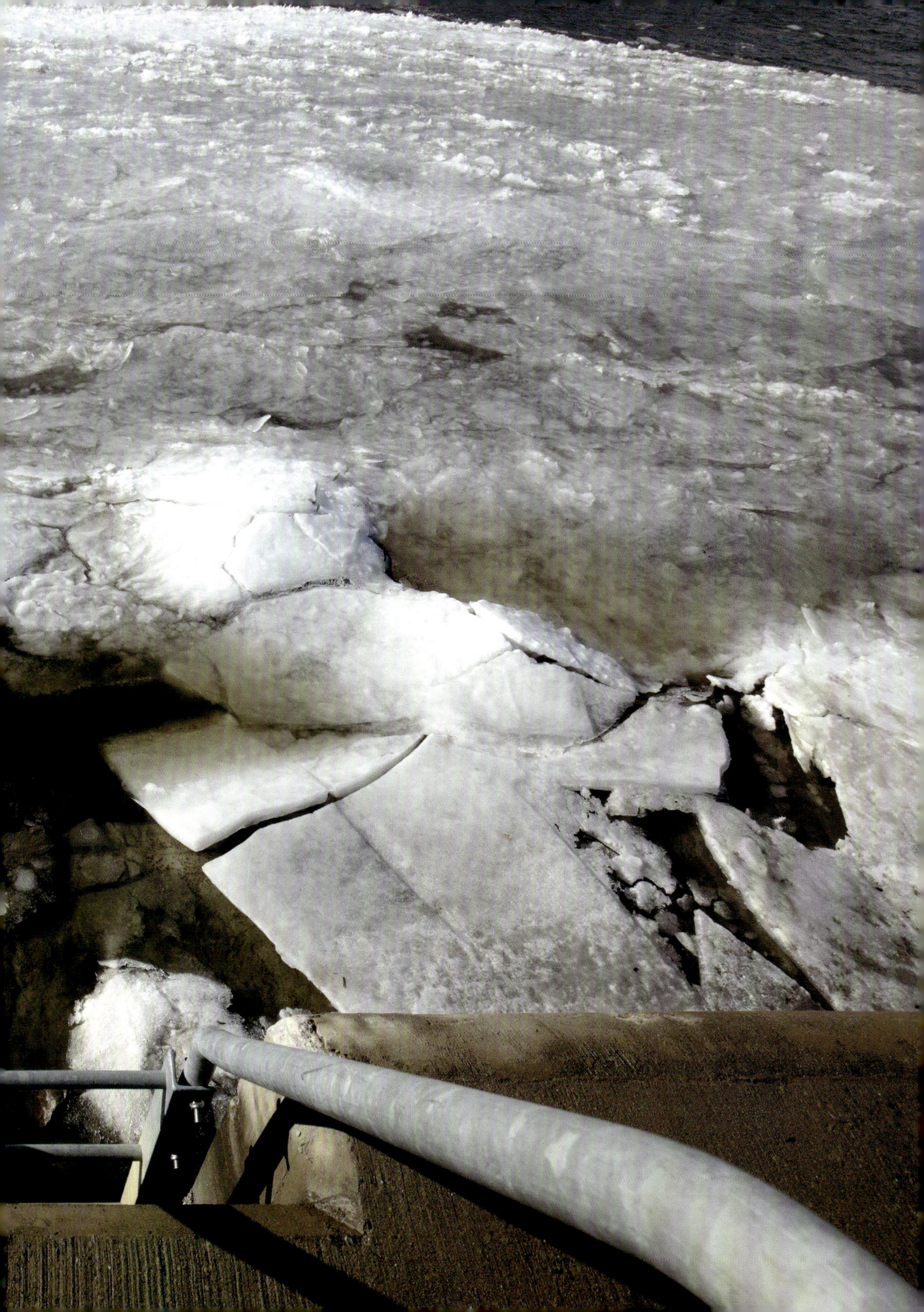

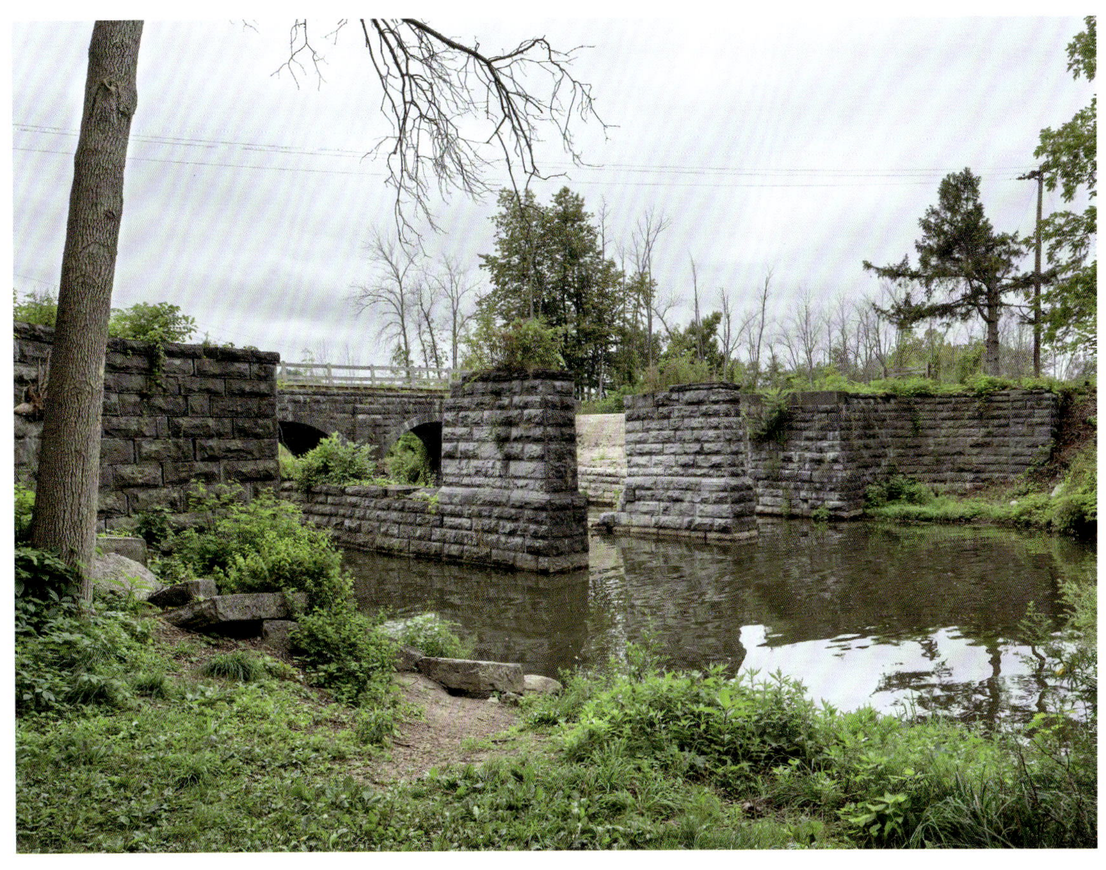

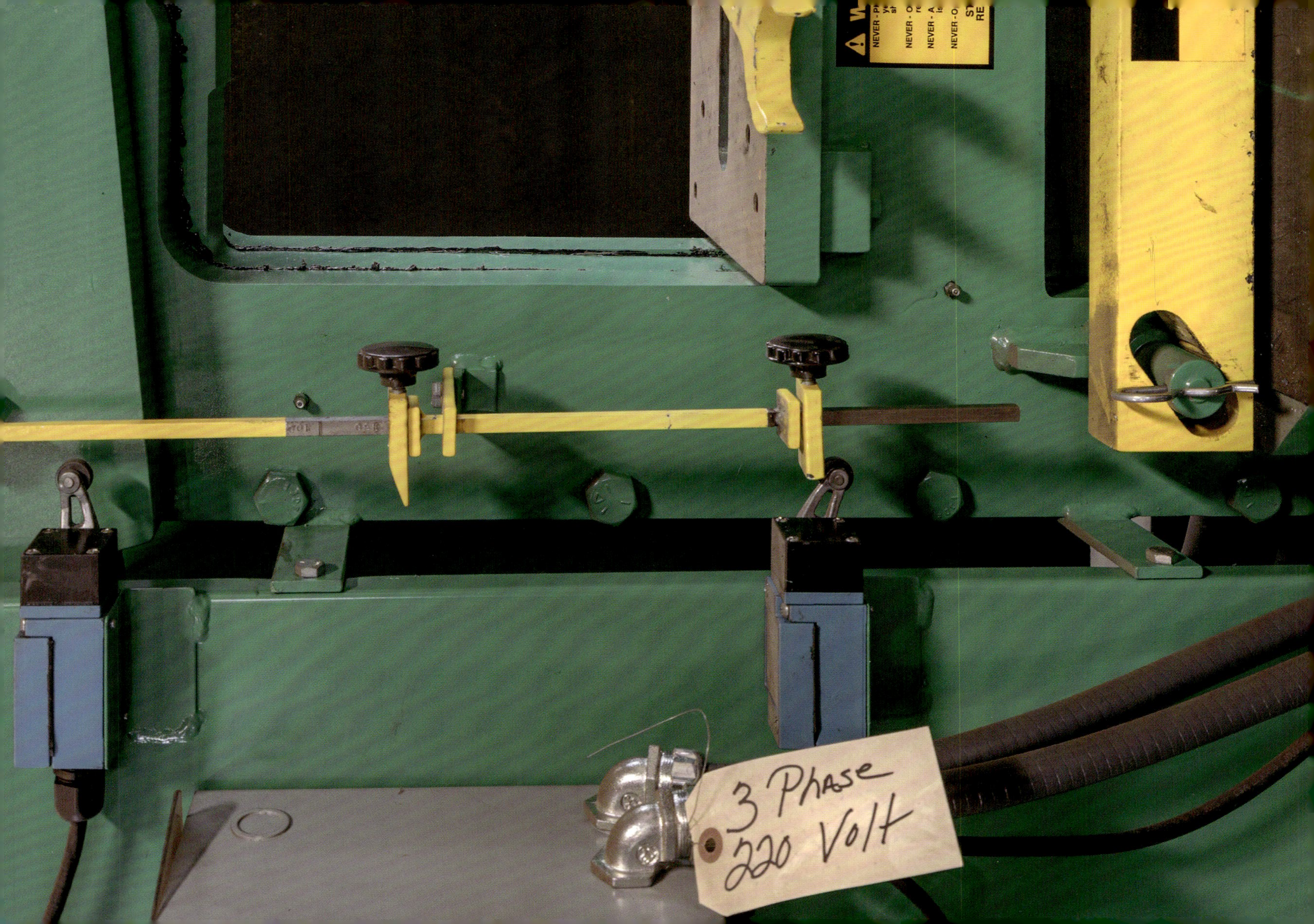

3 Phase
220 Volt

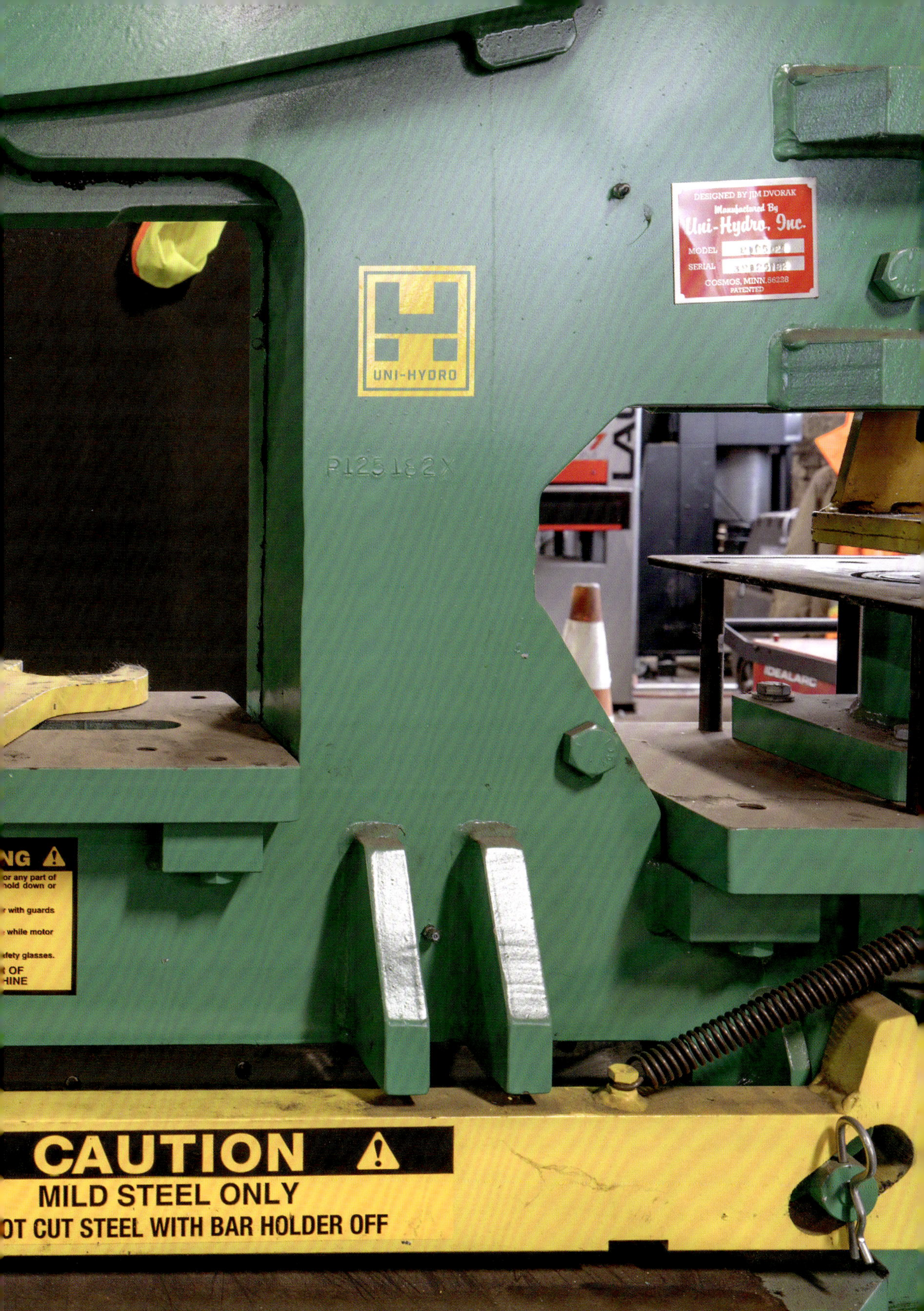
UNI-HYDRO
DESIGNED BY JIM DVORAK
Manufactured By
Uni-Hydro, Inc.
MODEL
SERIAL
COSMOS, MINN. 56228
PATENTED
CAUTION
MILD STEEL ONLY
OT CUT STEEL WITH BAR HOLDER OFF

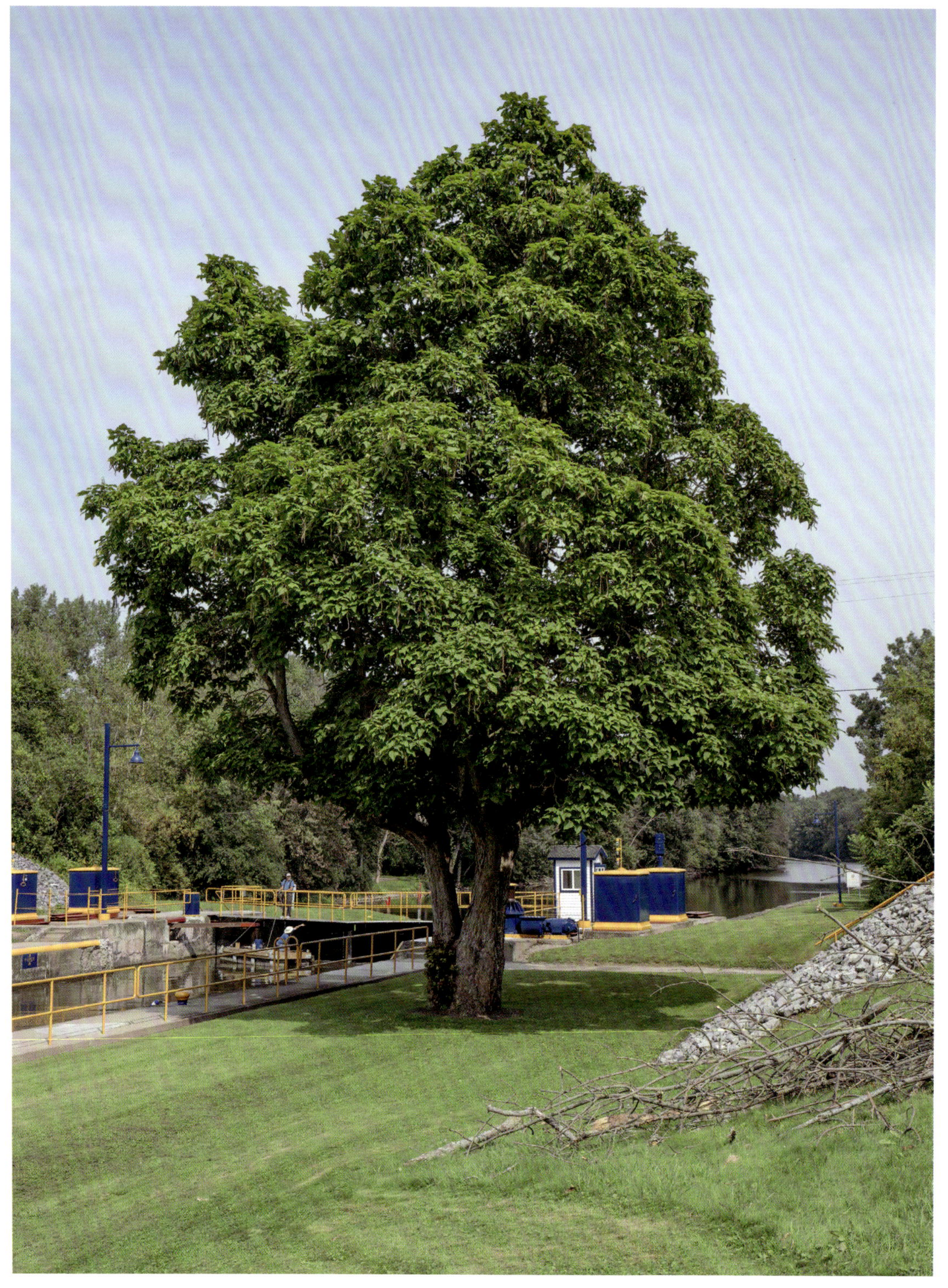

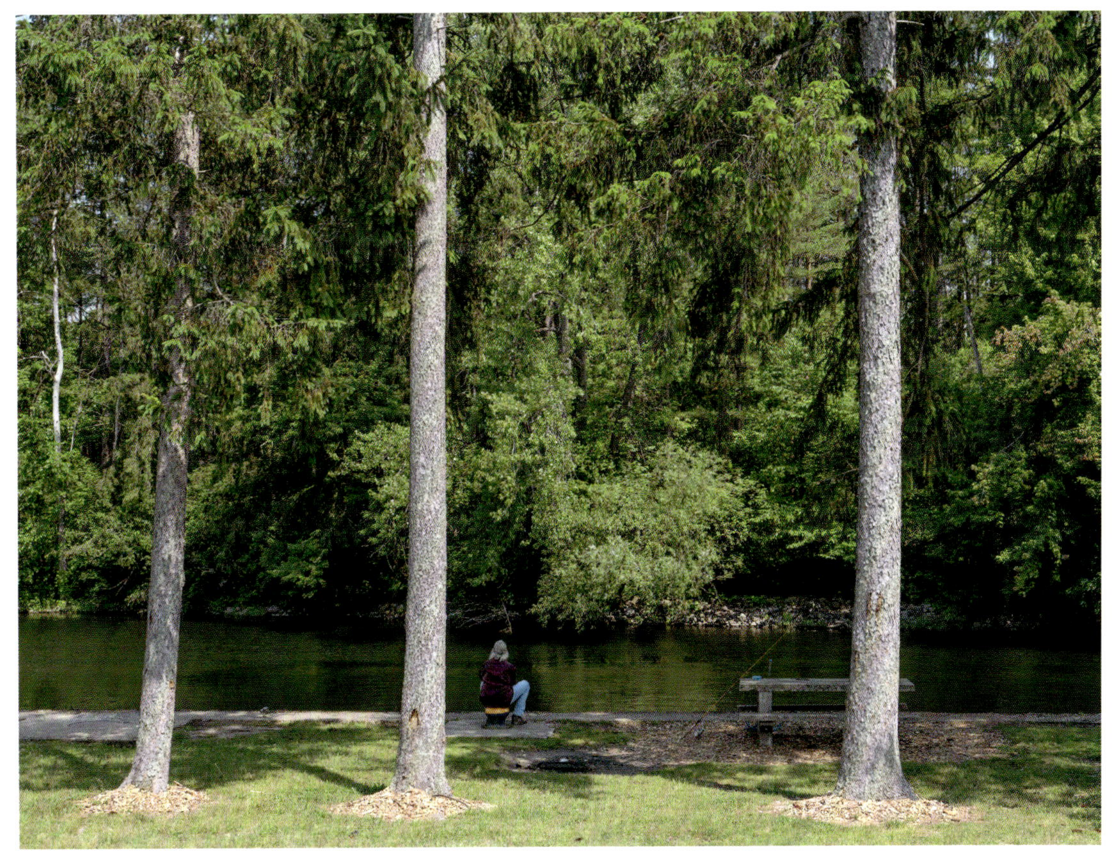

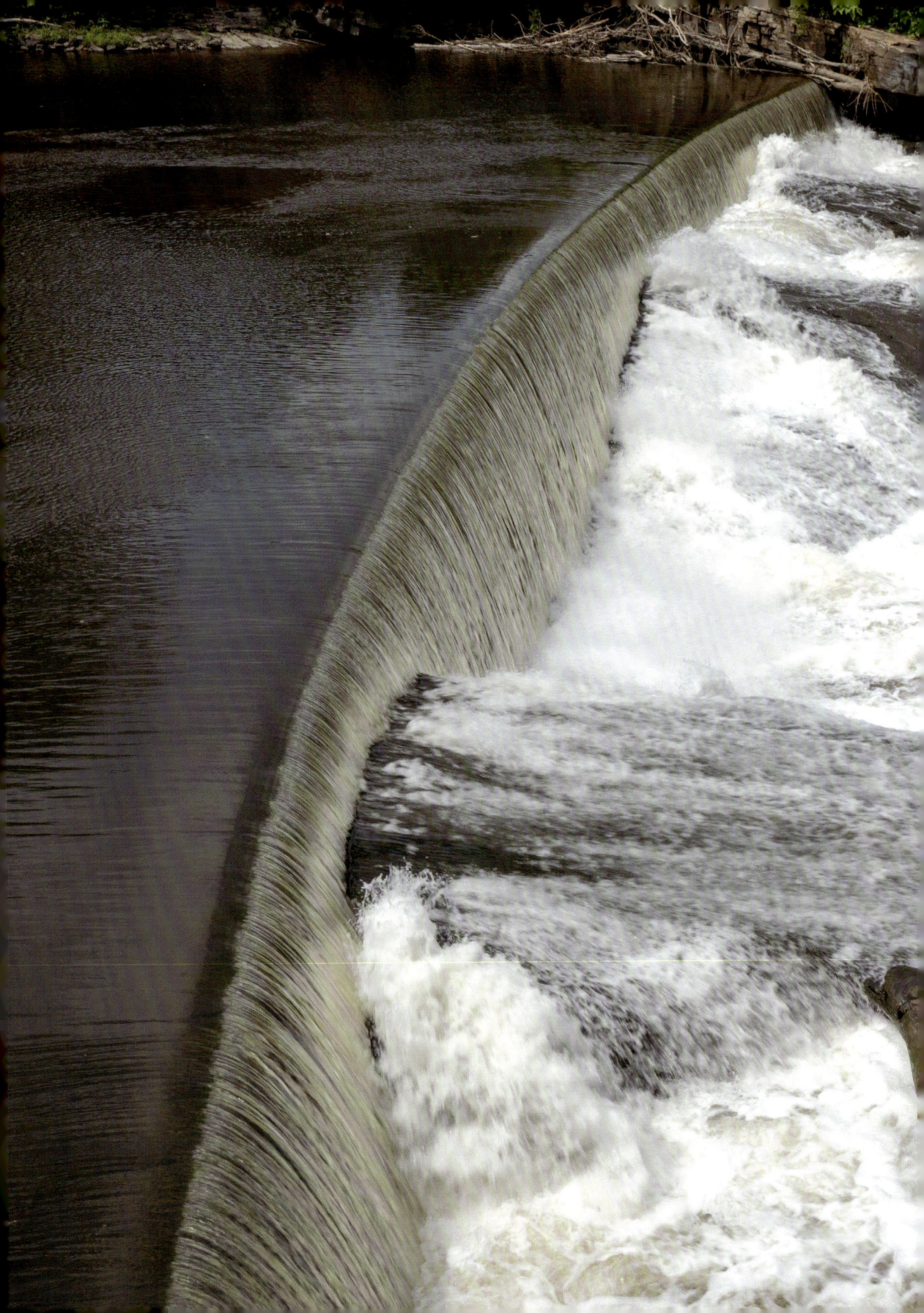

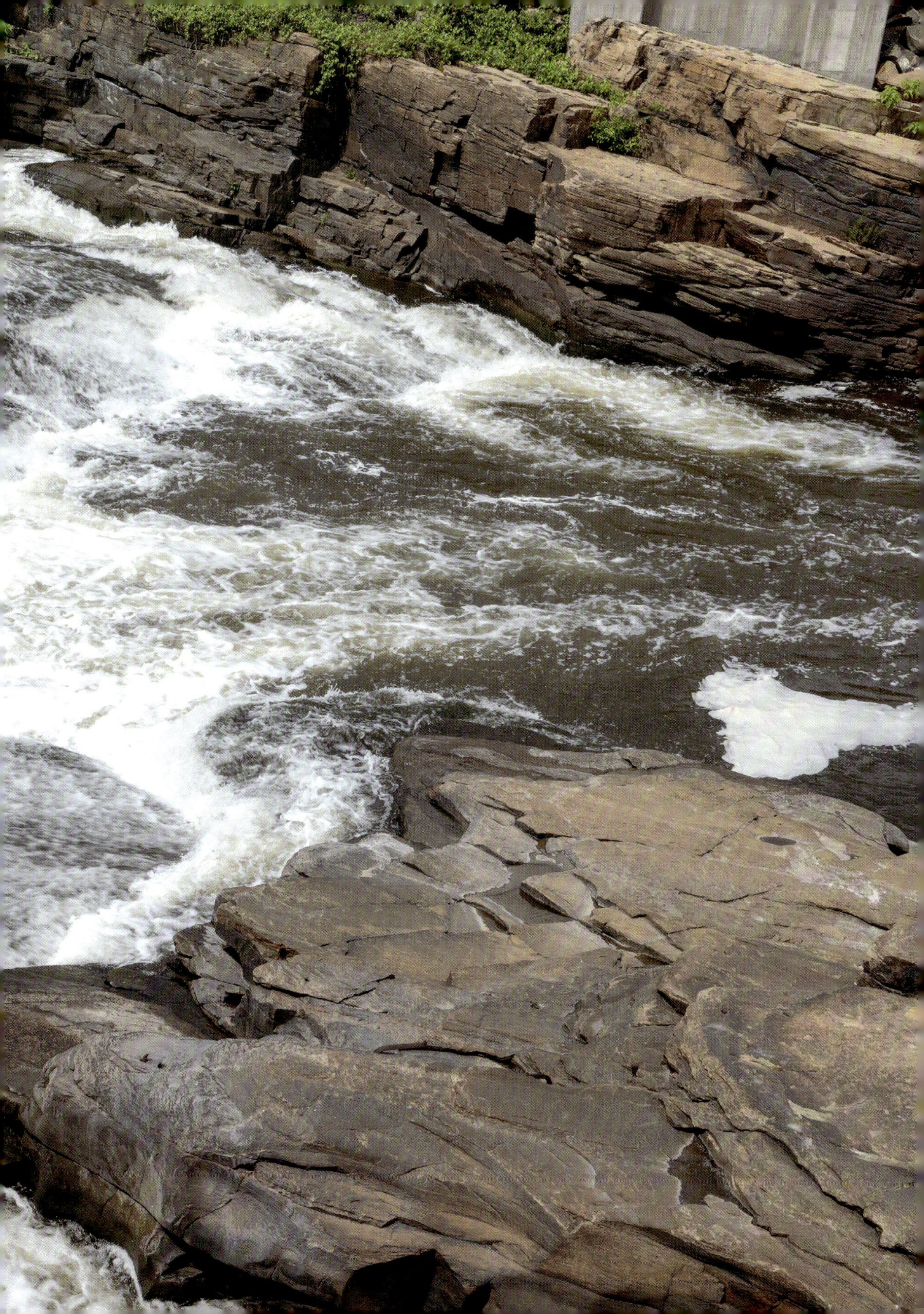

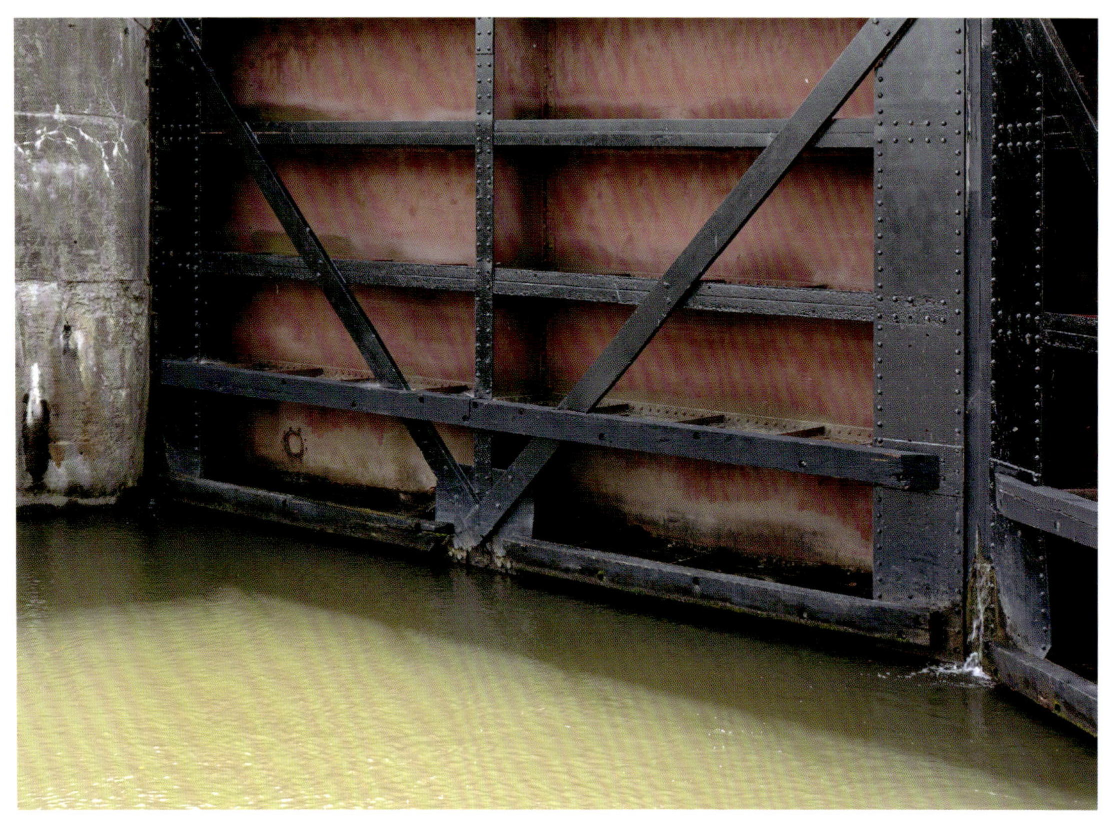

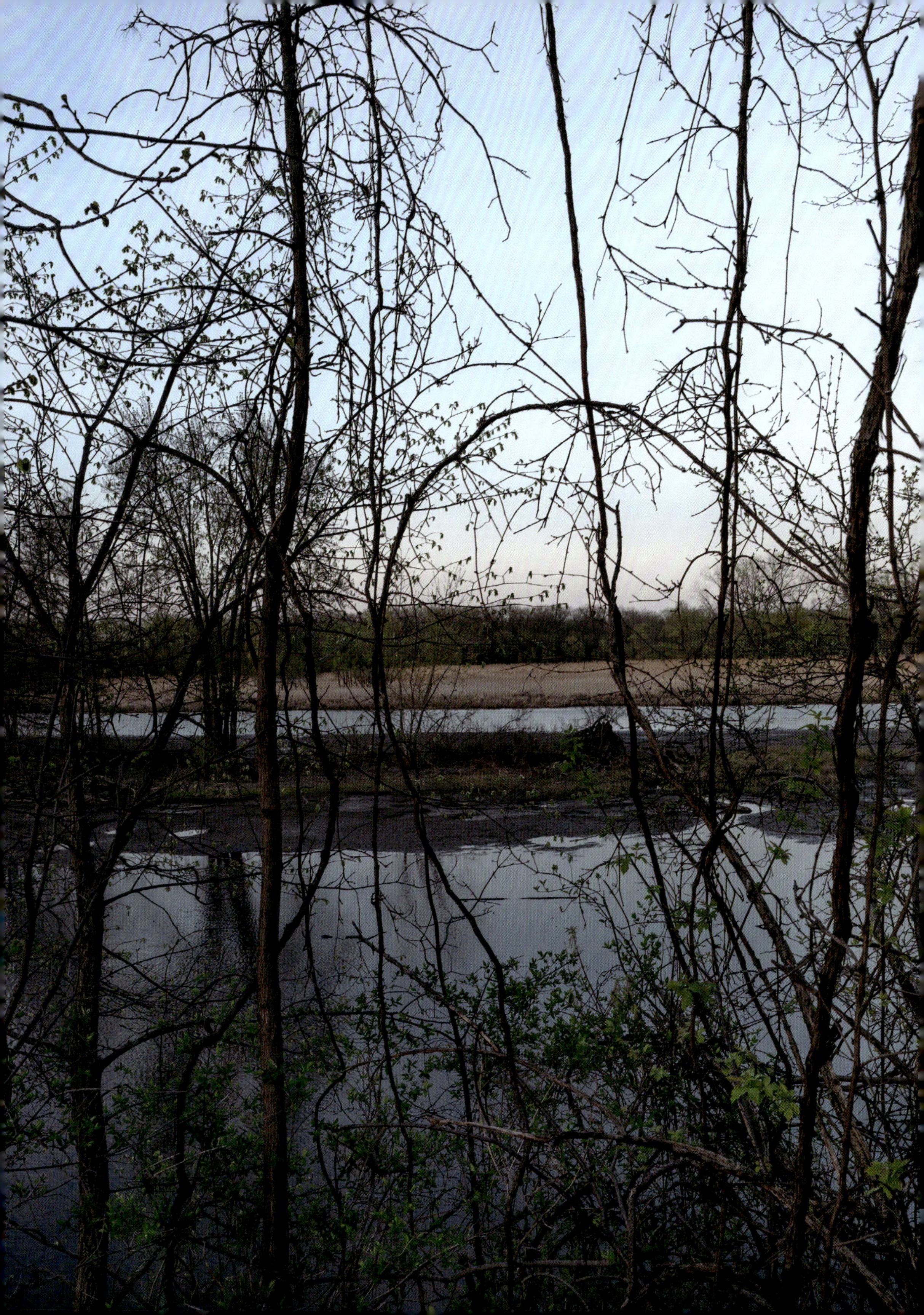

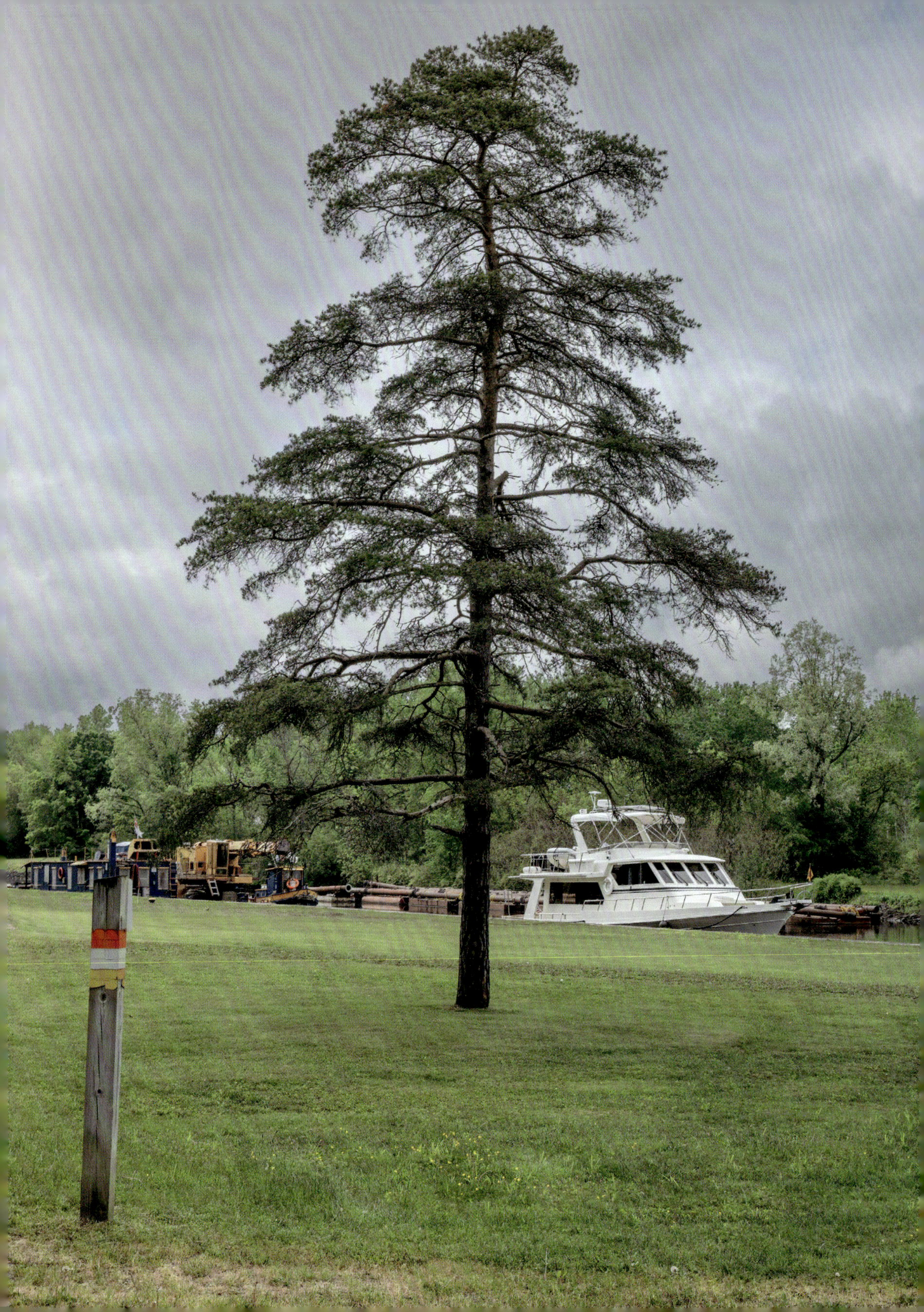

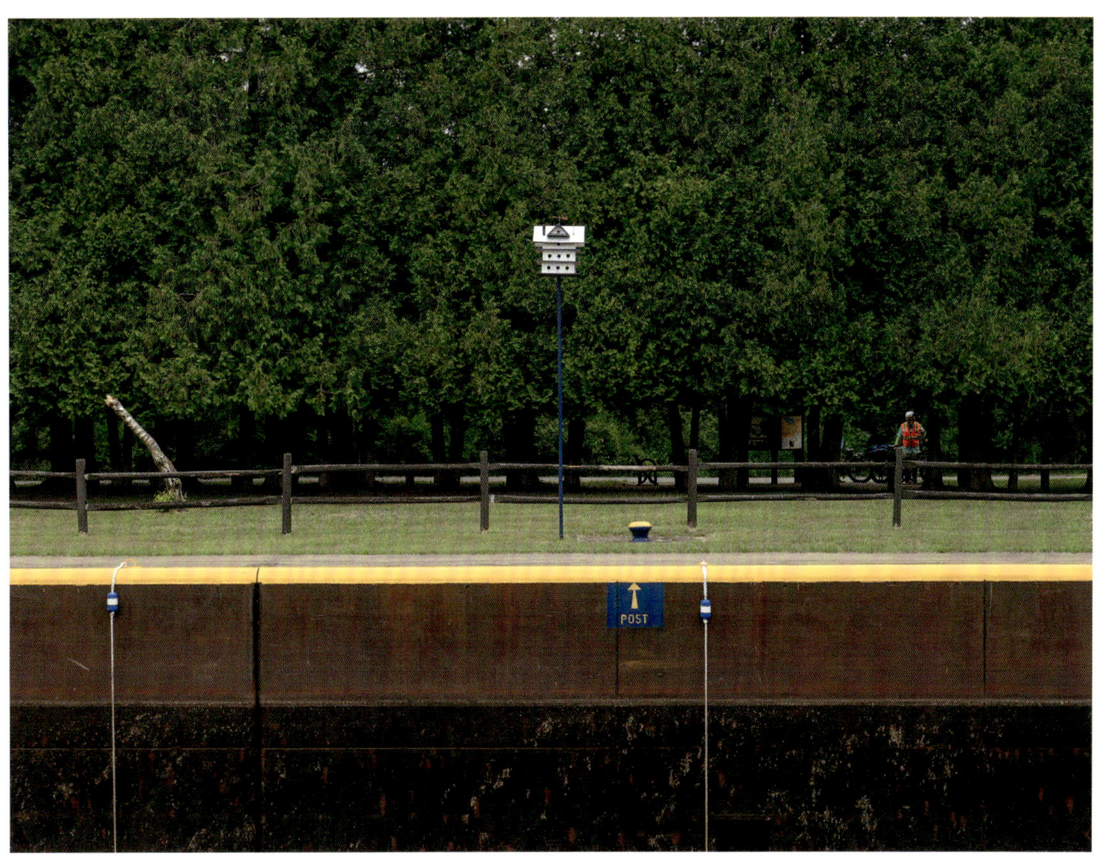
POST

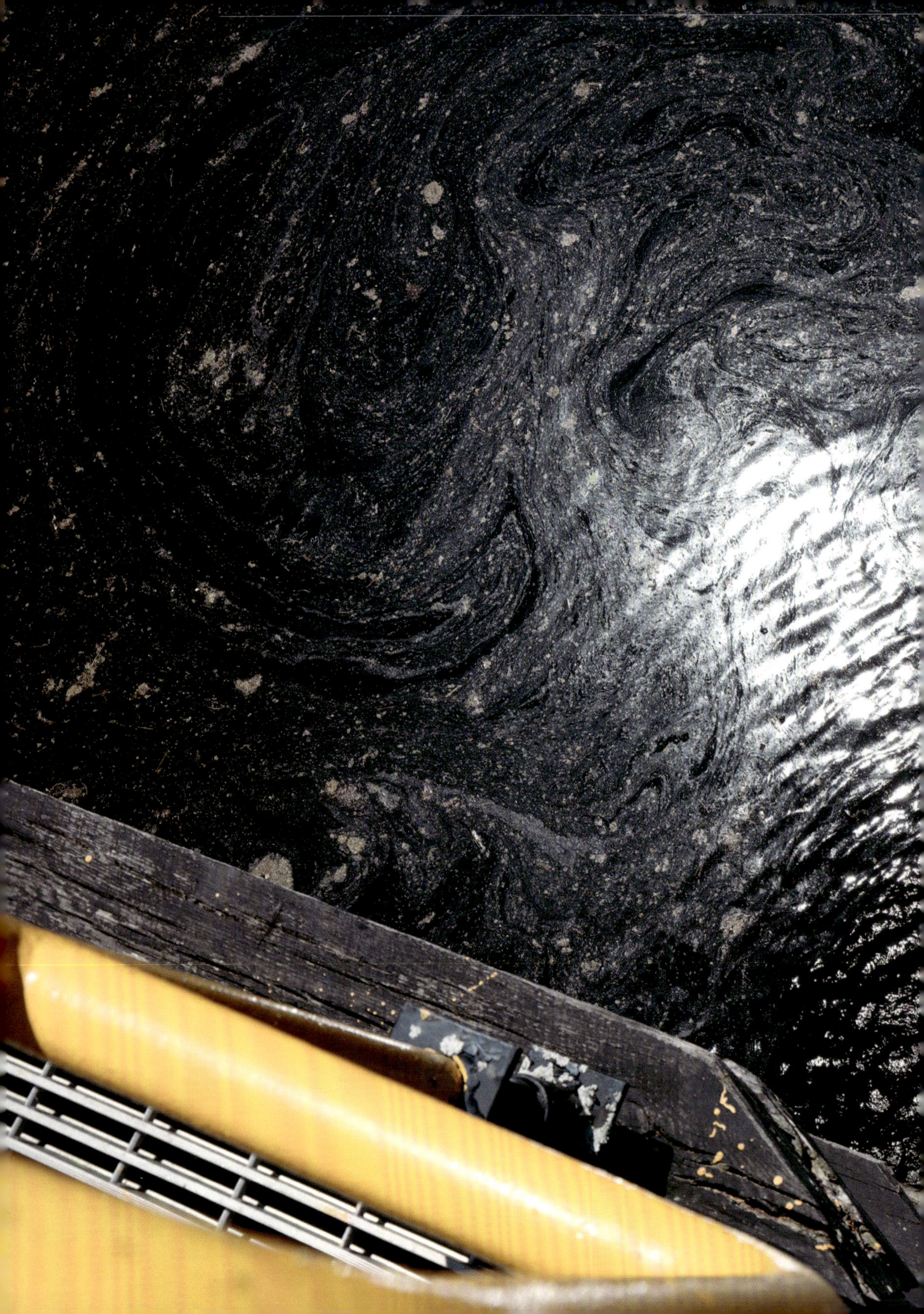

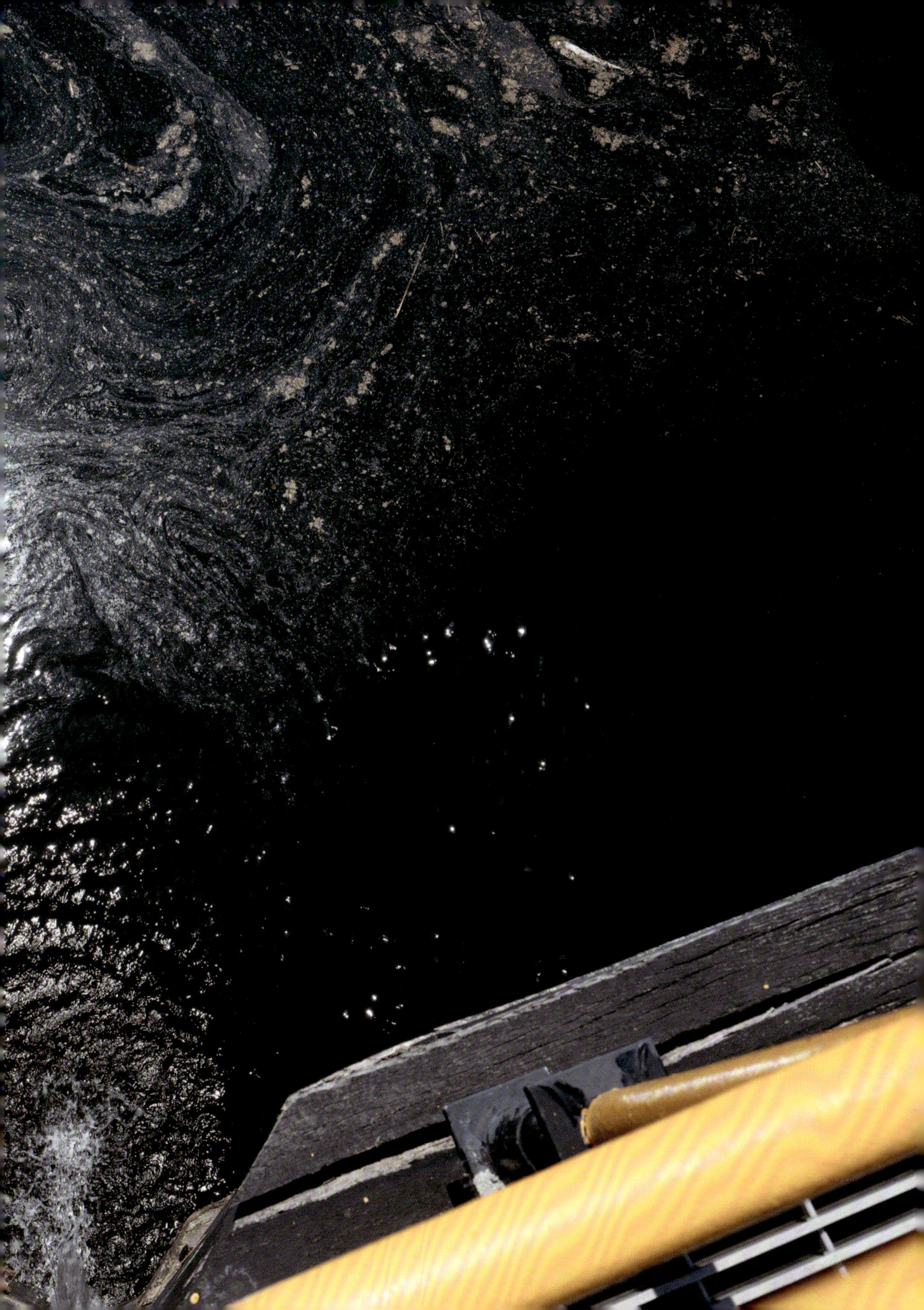

The Work and the Water

Matthew López-Jensen

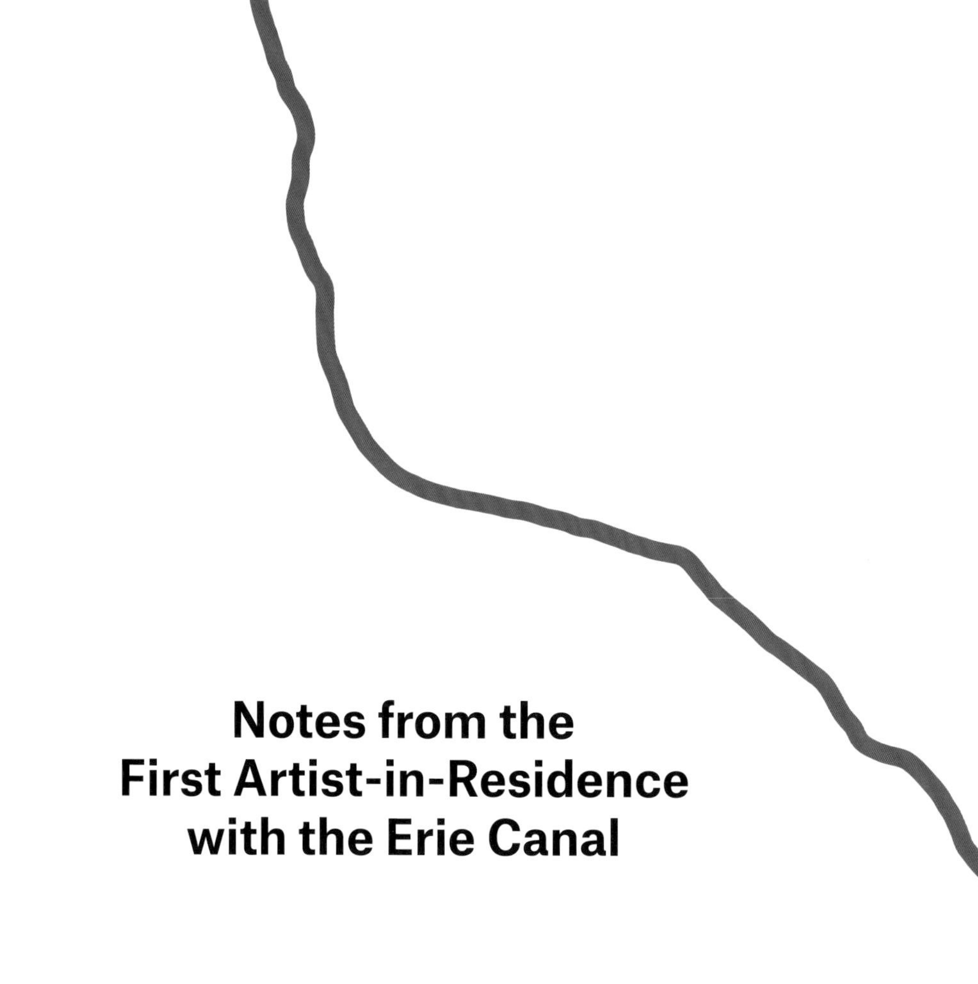

Notes from the First Artist-in-Residence with the Erie Canal

Lock 4 of the Champlain Canal in the town of Schaghticoke, New York, is also the confluence of the Hudson and Hoosic rivers. It is part of the 524-mile New York State Canal system and referred to in Canal shorthand as C4. I arrived in mid-May, a week before the start of navigation season at which point the fifty-seven locks in the Canal system begin operation and boaters commence their inland adventures. Over the previous four months I'd been steeped in relevant nonfictions and pulp fictions, historic maps, waterproof guides, travel brochures, canal blogs, and construction reports. I'd been on Zoom calls with staff from the New York State Canal Corporation, toured their offices in Albany, visited the Erie Canal Museum and its archives in Syracuse, and scuttled around winterized locks and movable dams. The research led me to a project highlighting canal maintenance and cottonwood trees (there's a connection, trust me). Part of my process would be to visit every lock, landmark, and point of interest in the entire system.

The Hudson River becomes the Champlain Canal just north of Albany at Waterford, New York. It is at this point that intermittent dams cross the entire river, controlling the water level and making navigation possible. The southern reach of the Hudson, from Albany to New York City, has no locks or dams, but connects the system to the rest of the world. Near the Erie Basin in the Red Hook neighborhood of Brookyn, if you were so inclined, you could find the perfect chair-and-table set for the deck of your boat at IKEA, install them while moored a few blocks away, and then enjoy a slow cup of coffee as you sail north. Once you reach Waterford, you can take the Erie Canal west to Lake Ontario or Lake Erie or continue north through the Champlain Canal. The Champlain, along with the Oswego and Cayuga-Seneca, are the three lateral canals that connect to the Erie Canal as it crosses New York State. Cruise north through Lake Champlain and you eventually reach the St. Lawrence River. From there, the world unfolds, and your next stop might be Black Tickle, Newfoundland. Had you gone west at Waterford, you might sail as far as Thunder Bay, Ontario, or Houston, Texas. You won't have been on the Erie Canal the entire way, but it will have made the journey possible. These might sound like far-fetched adventures, but there is a small contingent of proud "Loopers" who use the Erie Canal in this exact way.

It was a bright spring morning at C4 and I was alone, apart from the lock tender on a riding lawn mower in the distance. I noticed a footpath leading into the forest at the edge of the parking lot and decided to wander that way before visiting the lock. Immediately, I was among the trunks of massive cottonwood trees and a dense understory of freshly sprung ferns and mayapple. The path ended shortly at the bank of the Hoosic River. The water was especially blue, and a patch of rapids charged the air with energy and sound. I photographed a stand of calicoed sycamore trees at the edge of the river, their first leaves appearing among last year's dangling buttons. A silver maple, three small trunks growing from a larger, gnarled base, framed my view. I followed the edge of the river until reaching the steep face of a slate embankment painted with chalky lichens and glistening mosses. I photographed tufts of Quaker ladies knowing I would never do anything with the images; they represent my oldest memories of wildflowers. Locals had collected the driftwood that made up a land bridge over the embankment (to the best fishing spots no doubt). Before heading back to the lock, I photographed two enormous cottonwood trunks emerging from the ground like a pair of giant legs. I would continue to search for and photograph cottonwoods on my quest to visit every lock and point of interest along New York's canals. The trees thrive in recently disturbed land, they arrive first, grow fast, rebuild the soil, and stabilize everything. Cottonwoods are part of nature's maintenance crew.

Further north in Schuylerville, New York, at Lock C5, there is an old paddle boat moored at one of the docks. It looks operational but two full-size, model human skeletons in the cabin, one dressed as captain, the other as first mate, made me wonder if it was all just an inside joke, an elaborate nod to a bygone era. The infrastructure of Lock C5 looks much like Lock C4; in fact, much like nearly every lock in the system. There are railings and power houses, lock gates, retaining walls, ladders and life preservers, mowed lawns, and clear sight-lines, everything is meticulously painted bright white, navy blue, and goldenrod.

The landscapes around Lock C5 blend into Hudson Crossing Park, an active community hub with trails, a picnic pavilion, herb garden, stone labyrinth, and a large stage-like structure resembling the prow of an old canal barge. The combined landscapes form an island in the Hudson River. The trails lead to postcard views and the ruins of trolley and rail bridges. Most of the trees are cottonwoods, some of the largest I would meet and photograph in the coming months. One enormous specimen had recently fallen and the remaining trunk, still standing, had the portrait of an old, bearded man carved into it with a chainsaw. The trail ended in a grassy bank near the edge of the river with a curious homemade installation. A rotary phone was installed on a protected shelf, there was a small bench, a trellis, and several painted rocks. A hand-painted sign indicated that this was a "Telephone for the Wind" to speak to departed loved ones.

There are over four hundred people who work in the field to keep the 524-mile Canal system operational and most of the biggest tasks are done during non-navigation season (mid-October through mid-May). Every gear, rubber seal, socket, miter gate, and circuit board must, on schedule, be removed, stripped down, rebuilt, and reinstalled. Replacement parts, unique to the system, are milled in the Canal's maintenance workshops. Miles of cement retaining walls and stone embankments need to be repaired. Sediment must be dredged. Sink holes must be filled. Snags and fallen trees must be cleared. Working outside, along rivers, especially in winter, is punishing work. As artist-in-residence, I wanted to showcase this work side-by-side with scenic views of the system. I knew it would be impossible within my time and budget constraints to meet with every employee in such a far-flung system. I thought of Mierle Laderman Ukeles's *Touch Sanitation* piece where she shakes the hand of 8,500 sanitation workers. My workaround was to send every employee a letter that included a personalized note, a thank-you photograph, two hand-decorated blank cards for responses, and a stamped return envelope. I asked each employee to describe a challenging task or explain something that most civilians don't understand about the Canal. The replies trickled in over the summer months. I learned something new every time I opened the mail.

My last stop on the Champlain Canal on this day was Lock C6 in Fort Miller, New York. I noticed from a satellite view that there was a saw-toothed dam stretching across the Hudson River, it looked like the wide-open mouth of a shark. The lock grounds were snug, with a few picnic tables near a majestic southern view of the Hudson River. Pockets of the cement retaining wall had crumbled and filled with flows of vibrant stonecrop. I imagined my pictures of the succulents celebrated by botanists and lamented by the engineers.

The Canal cut the nearby neighborhood from the mainland and created Galusha Island. Around the bend from the lock was an old basketball court growing weeds and a baseball field with no visible diamond. The only signs of people using the landscape were subtle footpaths through stands of staghorn sumac leading to the eastern edge of the dam. I stood on a small landing and marveled at the geometry and harshness of this structure. Another footpath led me to an abandoned pump house. The signature goldenrod paint on the few remaining railings led me to believe it was once part of the Canal's infrastructure. Now it was the best place to stand and cast a line into the rapids at the base of the dam. A spray-painted memorial covered a chunk of amorphous steel, and other bursts of graffiti made this hulking form into a community art venue.

Three locks down, fifty-four to go. I also wanted to spend time in the different maintenance shops to photograph the machinery used to make parts for the system. And of course, I wanted to visit the ruins of the previous Erie Canal that runs parallel to this new (1918) version; the aqueducts, stone locks, tow paths, and small towns are all part of Erie Canal history. Then there were the lighthouses and piers in Cayuga, Seneca, Oneida, Erie, and Ontario lakes. Cohoes Falls, Niagara Falls, Rochester's High Falls, and all the falls in between were on my list. It was overwhelming, enough for several lifetimes worth of work. I had seven months.

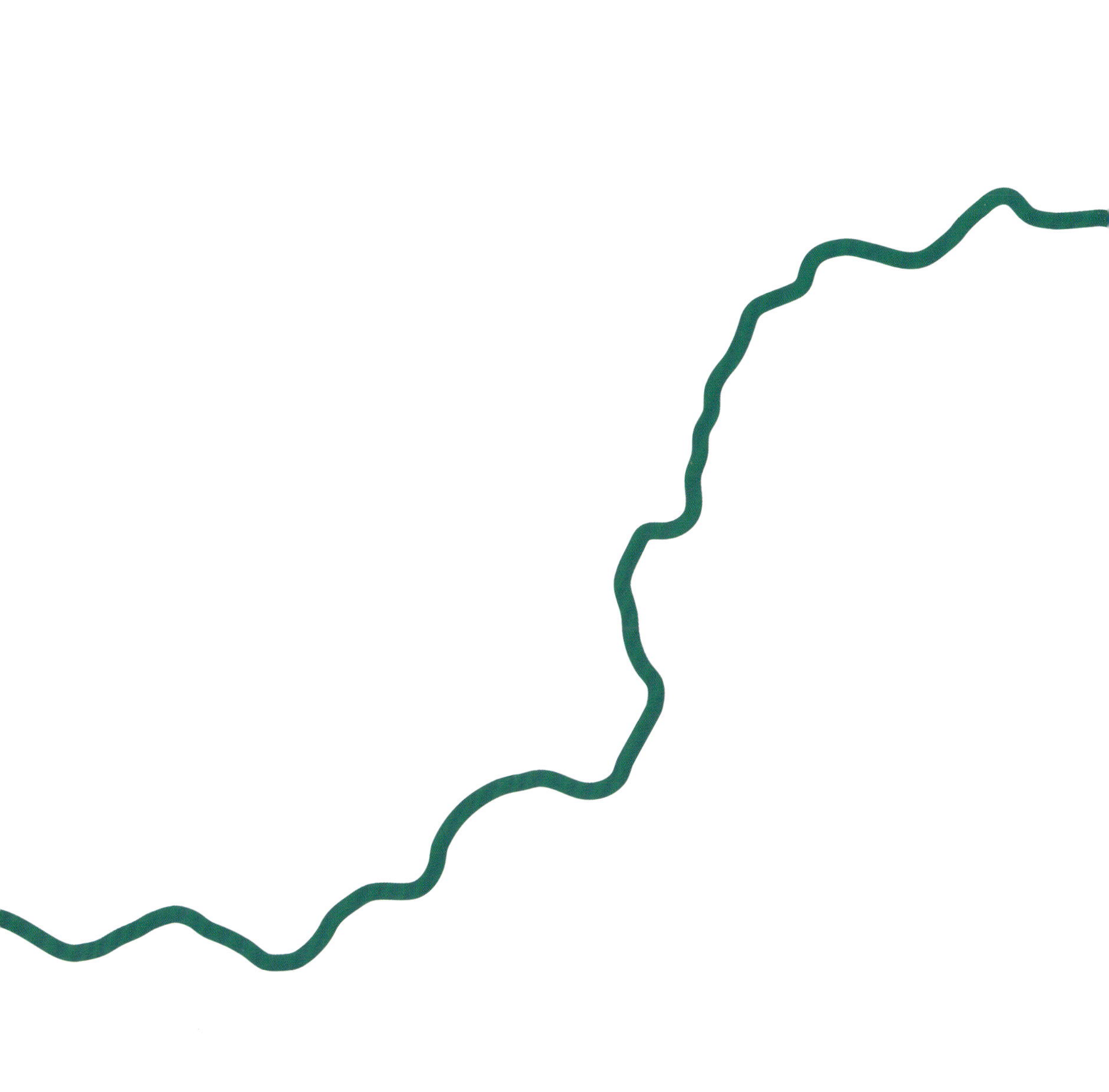

Image Index

Acknowledgments

I would like to acknowledge and thank the many individuals, groups, and agencies that made *The Work and the Water* possible.

Thank you to the many employees who work to keep the Canal functioning and accessible. Thank you to everyone who took the time to participate in this project and submitted notes about the work they do. I am honored to include these texts in this book. I'm thankful to all the section superintendents and supervisors who met with me at the start of this project and connected me with their teams. Thank you to the amazing team at the Canal Corporation for your direct support and assistance throughout the year.

Thank you to the Erie Canal Museum for supporting the research and development of this project, for fielding so many questions throughout the year, and for organizing the exhibition of work: Natalie Stetson, Derrick Pratt, Renée Barry, Elizabeth Farrell, Hannah Lewis, Amie Flanagan, Steph Adams, and Steve Caraccilo.

Thank you to the Horned Dorset Artist Residency in Leonardsville, New York, which provided me accommodations, amazing meals, and the resources necessary to spend time along the Erie Canal and its surrounding landscapes: Kingsley Wratten, Roberta Wratten, Aaron Wratten, Maddalena Molli, and Harold Davies. Thanks to my fellow artists-in-residence for their camaraderie, inspiration, and conversation: Myke Karlowski, Ira Mitchell, and Cindy Koren.

Thank you to my friend Peter Kostmayer for his infectious love of history as we visited sites from Buffalo to Rochester. Thank you to the many Canal community members who followed my @all524miles Instagram page and offered advice and commentary as the project progressed. Thank you to Kim Beil for her brilliant research and insight into the relationship between art and labor. And special thanks to my husband Jesús, who accompanied me on some of this adventure and edited everything I wrote along the way.

Thank you to Shannon Harvey, Adam Michaels, Zoe Kauder Nalebuff, and Ella Gold for the months of dialogue, the thoughtful design, and for giving this book a home at Inventory Press.

The Work and the Water was made possible by the New York State Council on the Arts with the support of the Office of the Governor and the New York State Legislature.

The Work and the Water was also made possible with additional support from the New York State Canal Corporation, Erie Canal Museum, and the Winifred & De Villo Sloan, Jr., Charitable Fund.

About the Contributors

Matthew López-Jensen lives in the Bronx and teaches environmental art at Fordham University and Parsons School of Design. IIe is a Guggcnhcim Fellow in photography with work in the collections of the Metropolitan Museum of Art, the National Gallery of Art, and the Brooklyn Museum, among others. He received his MFA from the University of Connecticut and BA from Rice University. He was the first Erie Canal artist-in-residence and has participated in residency programs at MacDowell, the New York City Urban Field Station, Guild Hall, the Queens Museum, Wave Hill, and L.M.C.C., among others. He is a Citizen Pruner, NYC Parks Super Steward, and community gardener.

Kim Beil is an art historian who teaches at Stanford University. She is the author of *Good Pictures: A History of Popular Photography* (Stanford University Press, 2020) and *Anonymous Objects: Inscrutable Photographs and the Unknown* (MACK, 2023). Her writing on photography and visual culture has appeared in the *Atlantic* and the *New York Times*, as well as in the *Believer* and *Cabinet* magazines, among others.

The Work and the Water:
Labor and Landscapes Along the Erie Canal

is published by
Inventory Press
2305 Hyperion Ave
Los Angeles, CA 90027
inventorypress.com

Copyediting and Proofreading
Eugenia Bell

Design
Ella Gold

Printed and bound in China through Asia Pacific Offset

ISBN:978-1-941753-77-4
LCCN: 2024945789

Distributed by
ARTBOOK | D.A.P.
75 Broad St, Suite 630
New York, NY 10004
artbook.com

This book has been made possible by the Erie Canal Museum
and the New York State Canal Corporation

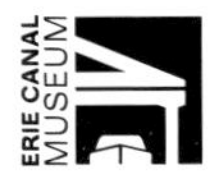

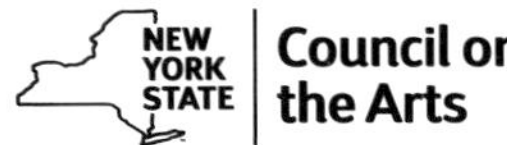

Winifred & De Villo Sloan, Jr.
Charitable Fund